I0454873

Congressional Research Service

Federal Pollution Control Laws: How Are They Enforced?

Robert Esworthy
Specialist in Environmental Policy

July 7, 2012

Congressional Research Service

7-5700

www.crs.gov

RL34384

CRS Report for Congress ————————————————————

Summary

As a result of enforcement actions and settlements for noncompliance with federal pollution control requirements, the U.S. Environmental Protection Agency (EPA) reported that, for FY2011, regulated entities committed to invest an estimated $19.0 billion for judicially mandated pollution controls and cleanup, and for implementing mutually agreed upon (supplemental) environmentally beneficial projects. EPA estimates that these efforts achieved commitments to reduce, treat, or eliminate 1.8 billion pounds of pollutants in the environment, primarily from air and water. EPA also assessed more than $152.0 million in civil penalties (administrative and judicial) and $35.0 million in criminal fines and restitution during FY2011. Nevertheless, noncompliance with federal pollution control laws remains a continuing concern. The overall effectiveness of the enforcement organizational framework, the balance between state autonomy and federal oversight, and the adequacy of funding are long-standing congressional concerns.

This report provides an overview of the statutory framework, key players, infrastructure, resources, tools, and operations associated with enforcement and compliance of the major pollution control laws and regulations administered by EPA. It also outlines the roles of federal (including regional offices) and state regulators, as well as the regulated community. Understanding the many facets of how all federal pollution control laws are enforced, and the responsible parties involved, can be challenging. Enforcement of the considerable body of these laws involves a complex framework and organizational setting.

The array of enforcement/compliance tools employed to achieve and maintain compliance includes monitoring, investigation, administrative and judicial (civil and criminal) actions and penalties, and compliance assistance and incentive approaches. Most compliance violations are resolved administratively by the states and EPA. EPA concluded 1,735 final administrative penalty orders in FY2010. Civil judicial actions, which may be filed by states or EPA, are the next most frequent enforcement action. EPA may refer civil cases to the U.S. Department of Justice (DOJ), referring 222 civil cases in FY2011. The U.S. Attorney General's Office and DOJ's Environmental Crimes Section, or the state attorneys general, in coordination with EPA criminal investigators and general counsel, may prosecute criminal violations against individuals or entities who knowingly disregard environmental laws or are criminally negligent.

Federal appropriations for environmental enforcement and compliance activities have remained relatively constant in recent fiscal years. Some contend that overall funding for enforcement activities has not kept pace with inflation or with the increasingly complex federal pollution control requirements. Congress appropriated $583.4 million for enforcement activities for FY2012, a decrease below the $593.5 million enacted for FY2011 and the $596.7 million enacted for FY2010, but an increase above the $568.9 million enacted for FY2009 and $553.5 million for FY2008. The President's FY2013 budget request included $615.9 million for EPA enforcement activities. To date, Congress has not completed action on the FY2013 appropriations for EPA.

Contents

Introduction... 1

    Federal and State Government Interaction 2

    Federal Funding and Staffing for Enforcement Activities... 3

    Other Enforcement Issues.. 5

Statutory Framework for Enforcement of Pollution Control Laws and Key Players 6

    Statutory Framework 6

    Key Players in Environmental Enforcement and Compliance 7

        U.S. Environmental Protection Agency 7

        U.S. Department of Justice.. 9

        Other Federal Agencies 9

        States and "Delegated Authority".. 10

        Tribal Governments... 12

        Citizens... 14

        Regulated Community.. 14

        Enforcement at Federal Facilities... 17

Enforcement Response and Compliance Tools... 18

    Monitoring, Inspections, and Evaluations 19

    Civil Administrative Actions 21

    Civil Judicial Enforcement 22

    Criminal Judicial Enforcement.. 22

    Sanctions and Penalties 26

    Penalties Assessed to Federal Facilities.. 28

    Supplemental Environmental Projects (SEPs) 29

    Environmental Justice and Enforcement/Compliance... 30

    Compliance Assistance and Incentive Approaches... 31

Funding for Enforcement/Compliance Activities 34

Conclusion 38

Figures

Figure 1. Key Players in Enforcement of Pollution Control Laws 1

Figure B-1. EPA Civil Judicial Referrals, Administrative Order Complaints, and
    Criminal Referrals, FY1992-FY2011 45

Figure B-2. Number of EPA Federal Inspections and Evaluations by Statute, FY1995-
    FY2011 46

Figure B-3. Environmental Enforcement Penalties Assessed by EPA: Administrative,
    Civil Judicial, and Criminal, FY1990-FY2011... 47

Figure B-4. EPA Supplemental Environmental Projects: Number of Projects and Dollar
    Value, FY2000-FY2011 48

Tables

Table 1. Major Federal Pollution Control Laws 6

Table 2. EPA Industry and Government Sectors 16

Table 3. Number of EPA Criminal Investigators: FY1997-FY2013 25

Table 4. Sector Web-Based Compliance Assistance Centers 32

Table 5. EPA-OECA's FY2010-FY2012 Enacted and FY2013 Requested Appropriation and FTEs by EPA Appropriations Account and Program Activity 35

Table B-1. EPA Civil Administrative, Civil Judicial, and Criminal Enforcement Actions, FY2006-FY2011 45

Table B-2. Number of EPA Enforcement Inspections and Evaluations by Statute, FY2006-FY2011 46

Table B-3. Environmental Enforcement Penalties Assessed by EPA: Administrative, Civil Judicial, and Criminal, FY2006-FY2011 47

Table B-4. Supplemental Environmental Projects (SEPs) Dollar Values as Reported by EPA: FY2006-FY2011 48

Appendixes

Appendix A. Enforcement/Compliance Databases and Examples of Reported Results 40

Appendix B. Examples of Reported Enforcement Actions and Penalties Over Time 44

Contacts

Author Contact Information 49

Introduction

Congress has enacted laws requiring individuals and facilities to take measures to protect environmental quality and public health by limiting potentially harmful emissions and discharges, and remediating damage. Enforcement of federal pollution control laws in the United States occurs within a highly diverse, complex, and dynamic statutory framework and organizational setting. Multiple statutes address a number of environmental pollution issues, such as those associated with air emissions, water discharges, hazardous wastes, and toxic substances in commerce. Regulators and citizens take action to enforce regulatory requirements in a variety of ways to bring violators into compliance, to deter sources from violating the requirements, or to clean up contamination (which may have occurred prior to passage of the statutes). Implementation and enforcement provisions vary substantially from statute to statute, and are often driven by specific circumstances associated with a particular pollution concern. Given these many factors, it is difficult to generalize about environmental enforcement.

This report focuses on enforcement of federal environmental pollution control requirements under the Clean Air Act (CAA); the Clean Water Act (CWA); the Comprehensive Environmental Response, Compensation, and Liability Act, (CERCLA or Superfund); and other statutes for which EPA is the primary federal implementing agency.[1] The report provides a brief synopsis of the statutory framework that serves as the basis for pollution control enforcement, including an overview of the key players responsible for correcting violations and maintaining compliance. Implementation and enforcement of pollution control laws are interdependent and carried out by a wide range of actors including federal, state, tribal, and local governments; the regulated entities themselves; the courts; interest groups; and the general public. **Figure 1**, below, presents the array of local, state, tribal, and federal entities that constitutes the environmental pollution control enforcement/compliance framework and organizational setting.

Figure 1. Key Players in Enforcement of Pollution Control Laws

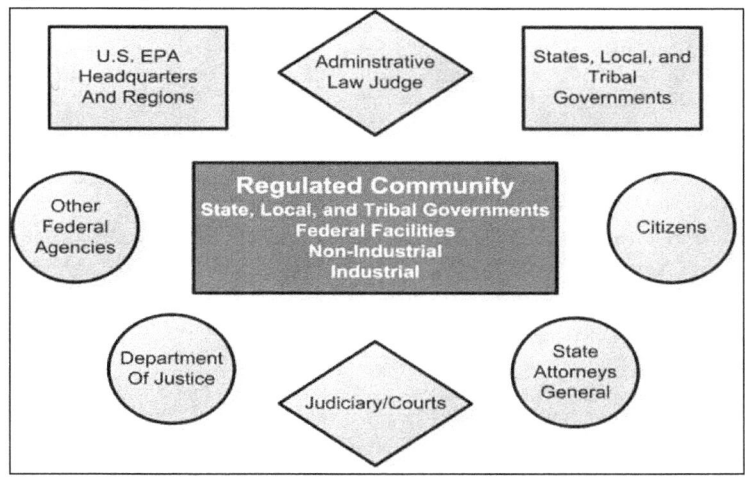

Source: Diagram prepared by the Congressional Research Service (CRS).

---

[1] See CRS Report RL30798, *Environmental Laws Summaries of Major Statutes Administered by the Environmental Protection Agency.*

A diverse set of regulatory approaches and enforcement tools is applied to a sizeable universe of regulated entities by these multiple regulating authorities to ensure compliance. A general discussion of enforcement monitoring and response tools is included in this report, followed by a summary of recent fiscal year federal funding levels for enforcement activities. Discussion of available enforcement data sources, as well as tables illustrating examples of trends in enforcement activities, is presented in the two appendixes.

While this report touches on many aspects of environmental enforcement, it does not describe every aspect and statute in detail. Rather, the report is intended to provide a broad perspective of environmental enforcement by highlighting key elements, and a general context for the range of related issues frequently debated. Information included in this report is derived from a variety of sources. These sources, including relevant subject-matter CRS reports providing in-depth discussion of specific topics and laws, are referenced throughout.

Several themes reflecting congressional concerns over time since EPA was established in 1970 are reflected throughout the major sections of this report. Congress has conducted oversight, primarily in the form of hearings, on various aspects of the organizational infrastructure and operations designed to enforce pollution control statutes.[2] These aspects of enforcement have also been the topic of investigations by the Government Accountability Office (GAO)[3] and EPA's Office of Inspector General (EPA-OIG).[4] The federal government's oversight of and coordination with states in implementing and enforcing federal pollution control laws have been of particular interest to Congress.[5] The following sections briefly discuss some of the key issue areas.

Federal and State Government Interaction

Since many, but not all, of the federal pollution control statutes authorize a substantial role for states, state autonomy versus the extent of federal oversight is often at the center of debate with regard to environmental enforcement. Not unexpectedly, given the "cooperative federalism"[6] that

---

[2] See, for example: House Committee on Energy and Commerce Subcommittee on Energy and Power, "*EPA Enforcement Priorities and Practices*," June 6, 2012, http://energycommerce.house.gov/hearings/hearingdetail.aspx? NewsID=9552; Senate Committee on Environment and Public Works, "*Oversight Hearing on EPA Regional Inconsistencies*," June 28, 2006, http://epw.senate.gov/hearing_statements.cfm?id=257928.

[3] Government Accountability Office (GAO): *Environmental Enforcement EPA Needs to Improve the Accuracy and Transparency of Measures Used to Report on Program Effectiveness*, GAO-08-1111R, September 18, 2008; *Environmental Compliance and Enforcement EPA's Effort to Improve and Make More Consistent Its Compliance and Enforcement Activities*, GAO-06-840T, June 28, 2006. All available at http://www.gao.gov.

[4] EPA's Office of Inspector General (EPA-OIG): *EPA Needs to Improve Its Recording and Reporting of Fines and Penalties*, Rpt. No. 10-P-0077, March 9, 2010; *EPA Has Initiated Strategic Planning for Priority Enforcement Areas, but Key Elements Still Needed*, Rpt. No. 08-P-0278, September 25, 2008; *Overcoming Obstacles to Measuring Compliance Practices in Selected Federal Agencies*, Rpt. No. 2007-P-00027, June 20, 2007 *Enforcement— Compliance with Enforcement Instruments*, Rpt. No. 2001-P-00006, March 29, 2001. All available at http://www.epa.gov/oig/.

[5] Ibid. footnote 3; see also GAO *Drinking Water Unreliable State Data Limit EPA's Ability to Target Enforcement Priorities and Communicate Water Systems' Performance*, GAO-11-381, June 17, 2011, *Environmental Protection Agency Major Management Challenges*, GAO-11-422T, March 2, 2011, *Environmental, Protection Collaborative EPA-State Effort Needed to Improve Performance Partnership System*, GAO/T-RCED-00-163, May 2, 2000, and *Environmental Protection Overcoming Obstacles to Innovative State Regulatory Programs*, GAO-02-268, January 31, 2002. See also EPA-OIG (http://www.epa.gov/oig/): *EPA Must Improve Oversight of State Enforcement*, Report No. 12-P-0113, December 9, 2011; *EPA Needs to More Actively Promote State Self Assessment of Environmental Programs*, Report No. 2003-P-00004, December 27, 2002.

[6] Many references discuss "cooperative federalism" in the context of environmental policy; these include Robert L. (continued...)

---

is often used to characterize the federal, state, and tribal governments in the joint implementation and enforcement of pollution control requirements, relationships and interactions among these key enforcement players often have been less than harmonious.

Disagreements involving environmental priorities and strategic approaches, and balancing the relative roles of compliance assistance with enforcement, contribute to the complexity and friction that come with enforcing national pollution control laws. Other contributing factors include the increasing number of statutory and related regulatory pollution control requirements (some with conflicting mandates) and the adequacy of the resources available for their implementation.

The effects of variability among statutes, coupled with variability in federal and state interpretations and regulations, are often central to the debate. Some argue that this variability leads to too much inconsistency in enforcement actions from state to state, region to region, or between federal versus state actions. Others counter that this represents the flexibility and discretion intended by the statutes to address specific circumstances and pollution problems.

A July 2007 GAO report found that progress had been made regarding federal oversight of state environmental enforcement programs, and that there had been improvements with regard to cooperative federal-state planning and priority setting. However, the GAO concluded that a greater effort was needed to achieve more consistency and effectiveness, and that these issues continue to need improvements.[7] More recently, in a December 2011 report, the EPA OIG found that although "OECA had made efforts to improve state performance and consistency ... state performance remains inconsistent across the country, providing unequal environmental benefits to the public and an unlevel playing field for regulated industries."[8]

Federal Funding and Staffing for Enforcement Activities

The level of federal funding allocated to states and tribes to support effective enforcement of federal pollution control laws has also been a long-standing congressional concern.[9] In March 2012, Environmental Council of the States (ECOS) reported concerns among state environmental agencies with regard to the extent of reductions in federal funding for state environmental

---

(...continued)

Fischman, *Cooperative Federalism and Natural Resources Law*, New York University Envtl. L. J. 179, vol. XIV 2006, Issue 1; Mark Agrast, et al., *How to Protect Environmental Protections?*, Envtl. Law Reporter, vol. 35, 2005 (10413 - 10417), the Environmental Law Institute; Philip J. Weiser, *Towards a Constitutional Architecture for Cooperative Federalism*, North Carolina L. Rev., vol. 79, 2001 (663, 671), University of North Carolina; Vickie L. Patton, *A Balanced Partnership*, The Envtl. Law Forum, vol. 13, no. 3, May/June 1996; and, Robert V. Percival, *Environmental Federalism Historical Roots and Contemporary Models*, Maryland Law Rev., vol. 54, 1995 (1141).

[7] GAO, *Environmental Protection EPA-State Enforcement Partnership Has Improved, but EPA's Oversight Needs Further Enhancement*. GAO-07-883, July 31, 2007, and *Environmental Protection Agency Major Management Challenges*, GAO-11-422T, March 2, 2011.

[8] *EPA Must Improve Oversight of State Enforcement*, Report No. 12-P-0113, December 9, 2011, http://www.epa.gov/oig/reports/2012/20111209-12-P-0113.pdf.

[9] For example, see EPA's Office of Inspector General, *Congressional Request on EPA Enforcement Resources and Accomplishments*, October 10, 2003, Report 2004-S-00001, http://www.epa.gov/oig/. GAO, *EPA's Execution of Its Fiscal year 2007 New Budget Authority for Enforcement and Compliance Assurance Programs*. GAO-08-1109R, September 26, 2008.

protection activities.[10] In a 2008 study, ECOS[11] reported that during 2005-2008 states expected spending to implement federal environmental laws to double while federal appropriations declined.[12] Subsequently, ECOS reported that although federal funding for enforcement allocated to states increased marginally from FY2009 to FY2010, overall, reductions in state budget revenue are impacting their ability to maintain viable environmental enforcement programs.[13] In 2007, GAO reported that, although funding overall for enforcement activities had increased somewhat, it generally had not kept pace with the increasing number of mandates and regulations, or with inflation.[14]

The federal enforcement funding and personnel, primarily within EPA and the Department of Justice (DOJ), to ensure effective enforcement of environmental statutes has also been a concern of both appropriations and authorizing committees in Congress. Recently, in addition to funding priorities among the various EPA programs and activities (including enforcement), several promulgated and pending EPA regulatory actions[15] were central to debates on EPA's FY2011 and FY2012 appropriations and are again prominent in the debate regarding the FY2013 appropriations.[16] During the previous fiscal year's appropriations deliberations, several provisions were proposed, and a subset adopted, that restricted the use of funding for the development, implementation, and enforcement of certain regulatory actions that cut across the various environmental pollution control statutes' programs and initiatives.[17]

Regulatory actions under the Clean Air Act, in particular EPA controls on emissions of greenhouse gases, as well as efforts to address conventional pollutants from a number of industries, received much of the attention during the FY2012 appropriations debate. Several regulatory actions under the Clean Water Act, Safe Drinking Water Act, and Resource Conservation and Recovery Act (RCRA) also received some attention. Some Members expressed concerns related to these actions during hearings of EPA's FY2013 appropriations, and authorizing committees continue to address EPA regulatory actions through hearings and legislation.

---

[10] ECOS Press Release: Prospects for Massive Cuts in Federal Funding Alarm State Environmental Agencies, March 26, 2012, http://www.ecos.org/.

[11] The Environmental Council of the States (ECOS) is a national nonprofit (501(c)(6)), nonpartisan association of state and territorial environmental commissioners, established in December 1993. http://www.ecos.org.

[12] ECOS, *March 2008 Green Report State Environmental Expenditures 2005-2008*, March 12, 2008, available at http://www.ecos.org/section/states/spending. See also, *The Funding Gap*, The Journal of the Environmental Council of the States, Winter 2004. http://www.ecos.org/section/publications.

[13] ECOS, *Status of State Environmental Agency Budgets, 2009-2011*, August 2010; *Impacts of Reductions in FY 2010 on State Environmental Agency Budgets*, March 2010; *Funding Environmental Protection State Budget Shortfalls and Ideas for Mitigating Them*, June 2009, available at http://www.ecos.org/section/publications.

[14] See footnote 7. See also, GAO Testimony: *Management Challenges and Budget Observations*, before the Subcommittee on Oversight and Investigations, Committee on Energy and Commerce, House of Representatives, GAO-12-149T, Oct 12, 2011, http://www.gao.gov/assets/590/585707.pdf.

[15] See CRS Report R41561, *EPA Regulations Too Much, Too Little, or On Track?*, by James E. McCarthy and Claudia Copeland, for a discussion of selected EPA regulatory actions.

[16] Appropriations Committees and several authorizing committees have held hearings to consider the President's FY2013 budget request for EPA, but no bill to fund Interior, Environment, and Related Agencies (includes EPA) for FY2013 has been introduced to date.

[17] See CRS Report R41979, *Environmental Protection Agency (EPA) FY2012 Appropriations Overview of Provisions in H.R. 2584 as Reported*, by Robert Esworthy. For an overview of proposed provisions contained in House-passed H.R. 1 and S.Amdt. 149, see CRS Report R41698, *H.R. 1 Full-Year FY2011 Continuing Resolution Overview of Environmental Protection Agency (EPA) Provisions*, by Robert Esworthy.

Other Enforcement Issues

Many other aspects of pollution control enforcement have been the subject of debate, and highlighted in congressional hearings and legislation. Some additional areas of continued interest include

- whether there is a need for increased compliance monitoring and reporting by regulated entities;

- impacts of environmental enforcement and associated penalties/fines on federal facilities' budgets (most notably the Department of Defense, or DOD, and Department of Energy, or DOE);

- how best to measure the success and effectiveness of enforcement (e.g., using indicators such as quantified health and environmental benefits versus the number of actions or dollar value of penalties);

- whether penalties are strong enough to serve as a deterrent and maintain a level economic playing field, or too harsh and thus causing undue economic hardship;

- how to balance punishment and deterrence through litigation with compliance assistance, incentive approaches, self-auditing or correction, and voluntary compliance;

- the effect of pollutant trading programs on enforcement; and

- the level of funding required to effectively achieve desired benefits of enforcement.

These issues result from disparate values and perspectives among stakeholders, but also from the factors that are the focus of this report: the statutory framework, those who work within this framework, and the tools and approaches that have been adopted for achieving compliance with pollution control laws.

The discussion below, beginning with identification of the principal statutes and key players, followed by an overview of integrated systems of administrative and judicial enforcement, compliance assistance, and incentive tools, is intended to provide a macro-perspective of environmental enforcement infrastructure and operations.

Statutory Framework for Enforcement of Pollution Control Laws and Key Players

As Congress has enacted a number of environmental laws over time, as well as major amendments to these statutes, responsibilities of both the regulators and the regulated community have grown. Organizational structures of regulatory agencies have evolved in response to their expanding enforcement obligations. Regulators also must adapt to an evolving, integrated system of administrative and judicial enforcement, compliance assistance, and incentive tools (see discussion under "Enforcement Response and Compliance Tools," later in this report).

Statutory Framework

The 11 laws listed in **Table 1** generally form the legal basis for the establishment and enforcement of federal pollution control requirements intended to protect human health and the environment.

Table 1. Major Federal Pollution Control Laws

Statute	Major U.S. Code
Comprehensive Environmental Response, Compensation, and Liabi ity Act (Superfund)	42 U.S.C. §§9601-9675
Clean Air Act	42 U.S.C. §§7401-7671
Clean Water Act	33 U.S.C. §§1251-1387
Safe Drinking Water Act	42 U.S.C. §§300f-300j
So id Waste Disposal Act/Resource Conservation and Recovery Act	42 U.S.C. §§6901-6991k
Oil Pollution Control Act (1990)	33 U.S.C. §§2701 et seq.
Environmental Planning and Community-Right-To-Know Act	42 U.S.C. §§11001-11050
Federal Insecticide, Fungicide, and Rodenticide Act	7 U.S.C. §§136-136y
Toxic Substances Control Act	15 U.S.C. §2601 et seq.
Pollution Prosecution Act of 1990	42 U.S.C. §4321

Note: This ist is not comprehensive in terms of all laws administered by EPA, but rather covers the basic authorities underlying the majority of EPA pollution control programs. For a discussion of these statutes and their provisions, see CRS Report RL30798, *Environmental Laws: Summaries of Major Statutes Administered by the Environmental Protection Agency.*

The discussion in this report focuses on these federal environmental laws for which the U.S. Environmental Protection Agency (EPA) is the primary federal implementing agency. Since EPA was created in 1970, Congress has legislated a considerable body of law and associated programs to protect human health and the environment from harm caused by pollution. Those federal statutes, intended to address a wide range of environmental issues, authorize a number of actions to enforce statutory and regulatory requirements.

Enforcement of this diverse set of statutes is complicated by the range of requirements, which differ based on the specific environmental problem, the environmental media (e.g., air, water, land) affected, the scientific basis and understanding of public risks, the source(s) of the pollutants, and the availability of control technologies. Regulatory requirements range from health and ecologically based numeric standards, or technology-based performance requirements, to facility-level emission and discharge permit limits. Several of the pollution control laws require regulated entities to obtain permits, which typically specify or prohibit certain activities, or delineate allowable levels of pollutant discharges. These permits are often the principal basis for monitoring, demonstrating, and enforcing compliance. In recent years, an increasing number of administrative initiatives have favored incentive-based regulatory approaches, such as trading of permitted emissions, which can affect the applicability of traditional enforcement approaches.

Regulating authorities establish enforcement response and compliance assistance programs to address the enforcement provisions of particular federal pollution control statutes. These environmental statutes typically authorize administrative, civil judicial, and criminal enforcement actions for violations of statutory provisions. For example, Section 309 of the CWA, Section 113 of the CAA, and Section 1414 of the Safe Drinking Water Act (SDWA) cover enforcement provisions.[18] As provisions for specific actions vary from statute to statute, each EPA regulatory program office establishes detailed criteria for determining what sanctions are preferable (and authorized) in response to a given violation. The statutes often provide a level of discretion to regulators for addressing specific circumstances surrounding certain environmental problems or violations of national requirements.

Enforcement of the many provisions of the major environmental laws across a vast and diverse regulated community involves a complex coordinated process between federal (primarily EPA and DOJ), state, tribal, and local governments. Congress provided authority to states for implementing and enforcing many aspects of the federal statutory requirements. Citizens also play a role in ensuring that entities comply with environmental requirements, by reporting violations or filing citizen lawsuits, which are authorized under almost all pollution control laws. The following discussion highlights the roles of these key players.

Key Players in Environmental Enforcement and Compliance

U.S. Environmental Protection Agency

Primarily through its program offices (e.g., air, water, solid waste), EPA promulgates national regulations and standards.[19] Other federal agencies (e.g., the Department of the Interior, Army Corp of Engineers) and states, tribes, various stakeholder groups, and citizens may contribute input to EPA at various stages of regulatory development (including required public comment). (States may also establish their own laws based on the national requirements; see the discussion later in the "States and "Delegated Authority"" section of this report.) EPA (and states) inform the regulated community of their responsibilities and administer permitting, monitoring, and reporting requirements. EPA also provides technical and compliance assistance, and employs a variety of administrative and judicial enforcement tools as authorized by the major environmental laws it administers, as well as incentive approaches, to promote and ensure compliance.

---

[18] See 33 U.S.C. §1319, 42 U.S.C. §7413, and 42 U.S.C. §300g-3.

[19] See CRS Report RL32240, *The Federal Rulemaking Process An Overview*, by Maeve P. Carey.

Since EPA's establishment, the agency's enforcement organization has been modified a number of times, and continues to evolve.[20] EPA's Office of Enforcement and Compliance Assurance (OECA) at headquarters and in the 10 EPA regional offices sets the general framework for federal enforcement activities in coordination with the agency's program offices, states and tribes, and other federal agencies, particularly DOJ. OECA serves as the central authority for developing and implementing a national compliance and enforcement policy, and coordinating and distributing policies and guidance.

EPA's National Enforcement Initiatives (NEI)[21] and OECA's National Program Managers (NPM) Guidance are primary strategic planning tools that set out national enforcement program priorities and coordinate and monitor state, regional, and EPA headquarters implementation of environmental enforcement/compliance activities. EPA's 10 regional offices, in cooperation with the states, generally are responsible for a significant portion of the day-to-day federal enforcement activities. The NEI is developed every three years with the cooperation of EPA regions and states/tribes, identifying overall program directions as well as specific enforcement activities/priorities. EPA is currently operating under the NEI for FY2011-FY2013, released February 22, 2010.[22] NPM Guidance is issued annually based on a three-year cycle coinciding with the NEI, identifying allocation of resources and expected outcomes, and serves as the basis for the enforcement agreements ("commitments") with the regional offices. The Guidance applies to OECA, all EPA regional enforcement programs, and states and tribes implementing EPA-approved inspection and enforcement programs. The Agency is currently operating under the FY2012 NPM Guidance was distributed April 30, 2011.[23] The FY2013 NPM Guidance was released April 30, 2012.[24]

The EPA National Enforcement Investigations Center (NEIC) provides technical expertise to the agency and states. The center administers an investigative team that assigns investigators to the regional offices as needed.[25] OECA also facilitates EPA's National Enforcement Training Institute (NETI), established under Title II of the 1990 Pollution Prosecution Act (P.L. 101-593). NETI provides a wide spectrum of environmental enforcement training online to international, federal, state, local, and enforcement personnel, including lawyers, inspectors, civil and criminal investigators, and technical experts.[26]

---

[20] For more information regarding EPA's current organizational structure for enforcement, see the agency's website at http://www.epa.gov/compliance/about/index.html. Several references describe the historical evolution of EPA, including Joel A. Mintz, *Enforcement at the EPA High Stakes and Hard Choices*, 1st ed. (University of Texas Press, Austin, 1995); and Clifford Rechtschaffen and David L. Markell, *Reinventing Environmental Enforcement & the State/Federal Relationship* (Environmental Law Institute, 2003).

[21] On February 22, 2010, EPA renamed its "National Enforcement Priorities" the "National Enforcement Initiatives," http://www.epa.gov/compliance/data/planning/initiatives/initiatives.html.

[22] *Ibid* footnote 21.

[23] EPA, FY 2012 Office of Enforcement and Compliance Assurance (OECA) National Program Manager (NPM) Guidance, April 30, 2011, http://www.epa.gov/planandbudget/annualplan/FY12_OECA_NPM_Gdnce.pdf. See EPA's "Planning, Budget Results" website at http://www.epa.gov/planandbudget/ for previous fiscal years' NPM Guidance.

[24] EPA, FY 2013 Office of Enforcement and Compliance Assurance (OECA) National Program Manager (NPM) Guidance, April 30, 2012, http://www.epa.gov/planandbudget/annualplan/FY13OECAFinalNPMGuidance.pdf.

[25] EPA's National Enforcement Investigations Center (NEIC) is located in Denver, CO. See http://www.epa.gov/compliance/neic/index.html.

[26] EPA's National Enforcement Training Institute (NETI), http://www.netionline.com/.

OECA's headquarters personnel conduct investigations and pursue or participate in national enforcement cases, particularly those potentially raising issues of national significance. More often enforcement activities fall to the regional offices. EPA (and the states') enforcement actions often require coordination with other federal agencies, most frequently DOJ.

U.S. Department of Justice[27]

In coordination with EPA, the Department of Justice (DOJ)—at its headquarters and through the U.S. Attorneys' offices around the country—plays an integral role in judicial federal enforcement actions of environmental regulations and statutes. EPA refers cases (including some initiated by states) to DOJ for an initial determination of whether to file a case in federal court. DOJ represents EPA in both civil and criminal actions against alleged violators, maintaining close interaction as needed with EPA, states, and tribes during various stages of litigation. DOJ also defends environmental laws, programs, and regulations, and represents EPA when the agency intervenes in, or is sued under, environmental citizen suits. EPA-OECA referred 232 civil cases to DOJ in FY2011 and reported 371 criminal cases were opened in FY2011[28] (EPA reported 168 criminal cases in FY2004 the last year criminal referrals were reported publicly by EPA)[29]. Many of these cases are handled by DOJ's Environment and Natural Resources Division (ENRD).[30] EPA and DOJ work conjunctively with the other federal agencies as cases warrant.

Other Federal Agencies

EPA and DOJ coordinate with a number of other federal agencies, particularly when taking criminal action. Key federal agencies include the Federal Bureau of Investigation (FBI), Department of Transportation (DOT), Department of Homeland Security (DHS, particularly the Coast Guard and U.S. Immigration and Customs Enforcement, or ICE), Fish and Wildlife Service, Army Corps of Engineers, Defense Criminal Investigative Service, National Oceanic and Atmospheric Administration (NOAA), U.S. Internal Revenue Service (IRS), and U.S. Securities and Exchange Commission (SEC). These agencies may provide support directly in response to violations of laws implemented by EPA, or, as is often the case, in circumstances where multiple laws have been violated.

---

[27] See http://www.justice.gov/.

[28] EPA-OECA, *EPA Compliance and Enforcement Annual Results 2011 Fiscal Year, December 12, 2011*, http://epa.gov/compliance/resources/reports/endofyear/eoy2011/index.html.

[29] EPA-OECA discontinued reporting criminal referrals beginning with reporting in FY2005. EPA, *National Enforcement Trends FY2004—Criminal Enforcement*, http://cfpub epa.gov/compliance/resources/reports/nets/report.cfm?CAT_ID=191&SUB_ID=1026&templatePage=3.

[30] EPA's cases are typically handled by three of the DOJ Environmental and Natural Resources Division's 10 sections: the Environmental Crimes Section, the Environmental Enforcement Section, and the Environmental Defense Section (http://www.usdoj.gov/enrd/About_ENRD.html). See also DOJ, *ENRD FY2011 Accomplishments Report Summary of Litigation Accomplishments*, http://www.justice.gov/enrd/ENRD_Assets/Accmplshmt_Stmt_2011_WEB_5_16_12b.pdf.

States and "Delegated Authority"[31]

Most federal pollution control statutes, but not all, authorize EPA to delegate to states the authority to implement national requirements.[32] For a state to be authorized, or "delegated," to implement a federal environmental program, it must demonstrate the capability to administer aspects of the program's requirements, including the capacity to enforce those requirements. Delegated authority must be authorized under the individual statute, and states must apply for and receive approval from EPA in order to administer (and enforce) federal environmental programs. While many federal pollution control laws provide authority for states to assume primary enforcement responsibilities, there is significant variability across the various laws, including as to standards states must meet and EPA's authority in determining whether states are authorized or have primacy. In some cases, state primacy is almost automatic.

Some federal pollution control laws limit the authority to a specific provision, while others do not authorize delegation at all. For example, Section 1413 of the Safe Drinking Water Act (SDWA) authorizes states to assume primary oversight and enforcement responsibility (primacy) for public water systems,[33] and Section 402 of the Clean Water Act (CWA) authorizes state-delegated responsibilities under that act to issue and enforce discharge permits to industries and municipalities. Under CERCLA (Superfund), states are authorized to participate in the cleanup of waste, from taking part in initial site assessment to selecting and carrying out remedial action, and negotiating with responsible parties. Under FIFRA, states may have primacy for enforcing compliance requirements contained on labels of registered pesticides, but are not granted enforcement authority related to registering pesticides or pesticide establishments. Programs under other laws, such as the Toxic Substances Control Act (TSCA), do not provide authority for state delegation. EPA can also authorize state government officials to conduct inspections for environmental compliance on behalf of the agency, subject to the conditions set by EPA, even if a specific statute does not provide delegation authority. However, there must be authority under the specific statute for authorizing such inspections.[34]

Even if delegation is authorized under a federal statute, states may opt not to seek delegation of a particular environmental program, or they may choose only to implement a select requirement under a federal law. For example, as of June 2012, 46 states had obtained the authority to operate the national permitting program under Section 402 of the CWA, but EPA had only delegated authority to two states to operate the wetlands permitting program under a separate CWA provision, Section 404.[35]

A majority of states have been delegated authority to implement and enforce one or more provisions of the federal pollution control laws.[36] Authorized states generally implement the

---

[31] The term "delegated authority" has become the most commonly used when referring to EPA's authority to approve states' programs. Federal statutes more often use "primary enforcement responsibility," "primacy," "approved," or "authorized" states' responsibility.

[32] See CRS Report RL30798, *Environmental Laws Summaries of Major Statutes Administered by the Environmental Protection Agency*, for references to sections of individual acts that provide state authority.

[33] See footnote 32, p. 48.

[34] See EPA guidance for issuing federal inspector credentials to state/tribal governments to conduct civil inspections: http://www.epa.gov/compliance/resources/policies/monitoring/.

[35] See CRS Report RL30030, *Clean Water Act A Summary of the Law*, by Claudia Copeland.

[36] The Environmental Council of the States (ECOS) has tracked delegated authority by state and statute; see http://www.ecos.org/section/states.

national laws and regulations by enacting their own legislation and issuing permits, which must be at least as stringent as the national standards of compliance established by federal law. States consider and approve environmental permits, monitor and assess environmental noncompliance, provide compliance assistance and information to the regulated community and the public, conduct inspections, and take enforcement actions. Local government authorities also play a role in permitting and monitoring. For example, EPA has delegated authority to implement Section 112 of the Clean Air Act (CAA) to at least three county governments. However, local governments generally act within the context of assuring states' requirements. For example, local authorities may incorporate land use and other issues as well as code requirements (fire, construction, building safety, plumbing, etc.) in their consideration of permits. A more detailed discussion of the many facets of local authorities is beyond the scope of this report.

A significant proportion of inspections and enforcement actions are conducted by the states. Comparable, comprehensive data from the same or similar sources are not readily available for purposes of directly comparing enforcement activities in states relative to EPA. While EPA routinely reports trends in its major enforcement actions in the annual OECA accomplishments reports and on its website, the agency does not include states' activities. There are a number of limitations with regard to states' information currently retained by EPA in its databases (e.g., not all states report relevant information into the EPA databases, reported data are not provided consistently from state to state, and reporting requirements are variable from statute to statute).[37] EPA is working to enhance and improve enforcement reporting by states. The agency has been implementing its State Review Framework (SRF) tool developed and introduced in 2004, to improve its oversight of state enforcement programs.[38] Under this SRF tool, EPA representatives visit and evaluate each state's compliance and enforcement program based on specified criteria.

Through discussions and reports, EPA provides feedback to each state and based on its review, outlines recommendations for improvement. Full implementation of SRF was initiated by EPA in July 2005 and the agency reported that reviews of all states and territories were completed in 2007. EPA began conducting Round 2 of reviews in 2008, and expects to complete these reviews in 2012. OECA, with its partners, conducted an evaluation of the implementation of the first cycle of SRF recommendations and initialed revisions to SRF guidance for conducting subsequent reviews. OECA continues to work with its partners in evaluating implementation of SRF recommendations.[39] Nevertheless, there are still perceived differences between states, EPA regions, and EPA headquarters.

In recent years, ECOS[40] has served as a forum to improve coordination and promote joint strategic planning between the states and EPA. In addition to other strategic planning tools, EPA and states established the National Environmental Performance Partnership System (performance partnerships, or NEPPS)[41] in 1995 in an effort to improve the effectiveness of EPA-state

---

[37] For example, see GAO report, *Drinking Water Unreliable State Data Limit EPA's Ability to Target Enforcement Priorities and Communicate Water Systems' Performance*, Report No. GAO-11-381 June 17, 2011, http://www.gao.gov/products/GAO-11-381.

[38] EPA-OECA, http://www.epa.gov/compliance/state/srf/index.html; see also EPA-OECA report *Best Practices and Program Improvements Expected to Result from SRF*, September 12, 2007, http://www.epa.gov/compliance/resources/reports/state/index.html.

[39] See footnote 24.

[40] The Environmental Council of the States (ECOS) is a national nonprofit (501(c)(6)), nonpartisan association of state and territorial environmental commissioners.

[41] See http://www.epa.gov/ocirpage/nepps/ for information regarding NEPPS.

coordinated environmental management. Under this system, which includes elements of compliance and enforcement, EPA and states enter into individual partnerships (performance partnership agreements) to address jointly agreed-upon priorities based on assessments of localized environmental conditions. The partnerships can be broad in scope or comprehensive strategic plans, and often serve as work plans for funding through EPA grants.

Absent delegation, EPA continues to enforce the federal law in the state, although a state can enforce its own environmental laws where not preempted by federal law. Even with delegation, EPA retains the authority and responsibility as determined by each statute to take enforcement measures, generally taking action when there is a violation of an EPA order or consent decree, or when the federal government deems a state to have failed to

> **Overfiling**
>
> The term "overfi ing" applies to situations when federal enforcement actions are filed during or after a state enforcement action against the same entity for violation of a federal statute. Some states and regulated entities use the term more broadly in reference to assertion of federal authority. Overfiling or the threat of overfiling sometimes strains EPA-state relations and cooperation, sometimes implying criticism of a delegated state's effectiveness.

respond to a major violation in a "timely and appropriate" manner. Additionally, when a noncompliance case involves an emergency or matters of potential national concern, such as significant risk to public health and safety, the federal government will typically intercede. There are cases where states request the federal government to step in, and other cases where the federal government on its own initiative acts on violations that are the subject of state enforcement action or settlement, known as "overfiling." EPA contends that overfiling occurs infrequently and that certain environmental statutory provisions preclude EPA from overfiling. These provisions are not explicit in all the pollution control statutes, and are limited to specific subsections and violations.[42] Although overfiling of states' enforcement actions has occurred under various pollution control statutes, historically, overfiling of Resource Conservation and Recovery Act (RCRA) violations has been the subject of considerable debate and litigation. States have strongly objected to overfiling, and the utility and extent of overfiling with respect to environmental enforcement has been the subject of considerable litigation, debate, and literature.[43]

Tribal Governments

EPA and states increasingly have recognized the role of tribal governments in environmental enforcement, where tribes, rather than states, have primary jurisdiction.[44] Indian tribes, as sovereign governments, can establish and enforce environmental programs under their own laws, but must obtain approval from EPA to administer federal environmental programs on their land.

---

[42] Provisions of the Clean Water Act (CWA) under §309 are often cited as an example of legislation limiting EPA's authority to overfile. EPA's authority to enforce under this section is only limited when a state has commenced an "appropriate enforcement action" in response to and within 30 days of EPA's issuance of a notice of violation to the state (33 U.S.C. §1319(a)(1)); when the state has "commenced and is diligently prosecuting" an action under comparable state law; or when a penalty assessed under a state-issued final order has been paid, the violation will not be subject of a civil penalty action under §1319(d) §1321(b) or §1365 (33 U.S.C. §1319(g)(6)).

[43] Ellen R. Zahren, *Overfiling Under Federalism Federal Nipping at State Heels to Protect the Environment*, 49 Emory L. J. 373, 375 n.18 (2000); Joel A. Mintz, *Enforcement "Overfiling" in the Federal Courts Some Thoughts on the Post-Harmon Cases*, 21 Virginia Envtl. L. J. 425, 427 (2003). Jeffrey G. Miller, *Theme & Variations in Statutory Preclusions Against Successive Environmental Enforcement Actions by EPA & Citizens, Part II Statutory Preclusions on EPA Enforcement*, 29 Harvard Envtl. L. Rev. 1, 3 (2005).

[44] EPA-approved/authorized state programs generally do not apply in Indian country.

As with states, some of the federal statutes authorize tribes,[45] with EPA approval, to assume responsibility for implementing certain federal pollution control programs. To obtain EPA approval, tribes must demonstrate adequate authority and jurisdiction over the activities and lands to be regulated. Where there is no approved tribal program, EPA exercises its federal authority and may undertake direct program implementation. In some instances, particularly when there are criminal violations, EPA may retain a role in compliance and enforcement even when there is an approved tribal program.

In addition to the federal statutes, a tribal government's authority for environmental protection can arise from federal executive orders, treaties, and agreements with the United States and/or state and local governments,[46] some of which explicitly reserve rights pertaining to the environment. When addressing environmental issues within tribal lands, EPA abides by the January 24, 1983, American Indian policy statement,[47] which reaffirmed the government-to-government relationship of Indian tribes with the United States.[48]

Relatively few tribes have obtained authority for implementing federal pollution control laws, and EPA identified tribal environmental compliance as a national enforcement and compliance priority in its FY2005-FY2007 and its FY2008-FY2011[49]enforcement strategic plans in an effort to enhance tribal governments' capabilities to implement federal environmental statutes. The primary focus was public drinking water systems, federal pollution control statutes applicable to schools, and unregulated dumping of solid waste. EPA's National Enforcement Initiatives for FY2011-FY2013 did not designate Indian Country as one of the six national enforcement initiatives, however, the sector will continue to be addressed through the structure established under the previous designated initiative or through the regular program compliance assistance, inspections, investigations, and enforcement conducted in regional offices and states.[50] EPA indicated that, during FY2011, EPA regions continued to provide compliance assistance, conduct compliance monitoring, and take enforcement in Indian country, particularly in the drinking water area.[51]

---

[45] Some pollution control laws have been amended to clarify the role of tribal governments in the implementation of federal environmental programs. For example, from 1986 to 1990, Congress amended the Clean Water Act (33 U.S.C. §1377(e)(2)), Safe Drinking Water Act (42 U.S.C. §300j-11(b)(1)(B)), and Clean Air Act (42 U.S.C. §7601(d)(2)(B) to authorize EPA to treat Indian tribes in the same manner as states for purposes of program authorization.

[46] For example, see Executive Order No. 13175 on Consultation and Coordination With Indian Tribal Governments, 65 *Federal Register* 67249 (November 9, 2000); Executive Memorandum on Government-to-Government Relations with Native American Tribal Governments, April 29, 1994.

[47] Issued by President Ronald Reagan, the policy expanded the 1970 national Indian policy of self-determination for tribes, http://www.epa.gov/tribalportal/basicinfo/presidential-docs.html.

[48] In conjunction with the 1983 overall federal policy statement, EPA consolidated existing agency statements into a single policy statement to ensure consistency. See *EPA Policy for the Administration of Environmental Programs on Indian Reservations*, http://www.epa.gov/superfund/community/relocation/policy.htm.

[49] EPA-OECA, National Enforcement Initiative for Fiscal years 2008-2010 *Indian Country*, http://www.epa.gov/compliance/data/planning/priorities/tribal.html.

[50] EPA-OECA, National Enforcement Initiatives, http://www.epa.gov/compliance/data/planning/initiatives/index.html.

[51] EPA-OECA, National Enforcement Initiative for Fiscal years 2008-2010 *Indian Country: Transition to the FY 2011-2013 National Enforcement Initiatives*, http://www.epa.gov/compliance/data/planning/priorities/tribal.html.

Citizens

Private individuals play an important role in enforcing certain aspects of federal pollution control laws. Citizen participation, specifically authorized by Congress in many of the federal pollution control statutes, occurs in several ways. Individuals can identify and report violations of the laws, provide comments on settlements that are reached between the federal government and violators of the environmental laws in enforcement cases, and initiate enforcement proceedings directly in response to alleged violations. In addition, individuals may bring actions against EPA for failing to execute nondiscretionary duties required under federal environmental laws.[52]

To further enhance public participation and reporting of potential environmental violations, EPA-OECA introduced the "National Report a Violation" website in January 2006.[53] The website provides access to OECA's online citizens' tips and complaints form. EPA reported that the number of citizen tips and complaints increased from 1,485 in FY2005 to 3,274 in FY2006. According to EPA, more than 18,000 total tips were reported to date, including more than 7,800 received in FY2008[54] (not reported for FY2009 through FY2011). Additionally, in FY2009 EPA introduced the "EPA Fugitives" website to solicit public assistance in locating alleged environmental criminal fugitives. (See brief overview of the website in the "Criminal Judicial Enforcement" section of this report.)

Regulated Community

The size and diversity of the regulated community are vast, spanning numerous industrial and nonindustrial entities, small and large, and their operations. The following discussion provides an overview of the regulated community, and highlights the role and activities of the key regulated entities in the enforcement of the primary pollution control statutes.

The universe of the regulated community as a whole is very large (see discussion below). The majority of those in the regulated community are required to comply with multiple statutes because of the nature of their activities and operations. The regulated community includes a diverse range of entities and operations, including utilities, refineries, manufacturing and processing facilities, agriculture producers and processors, mobile sources (e.g., private and commercial vehicles), and others. Local, state, tribal, and federal governments are also part of the regulated community, as they are engaged in a range of activities and operations—utilities, construction, waste and wastewater management, drinking water management, transportation, and pest management—that generate pollution similar to nongovernment sectors.

Regulated entities vary in their activities and operations, and in size—ranging from small individual business operations such as dry-cleaners to facilities and operations that are part of large corporations and conglomerates. Regulatory agencies generally categorize regulated entities into minor and major emitters/dischargers based on factors such as total earnings, number of employees, production volume, and amount of emissions, for purposes of implementing and

---

[52] Although not strictly speaking "enforcement," citizens may also petition for review of agency actions under a program statute or the Administrative Procedure Act.

[53] EPA-OECA, *Report an Environmental Violation*, http://www.epa.gov/tips. See also *Report Spills and Environmental Violations*, http://www.epa.gov/epahome/violations.htm#who.

[54] EPA-OECA, *Compliance and Enforcement Annual Results FY2008 Report a Violation*, http://www.epa.gov/compliance/resources/reports/endofyear/eoy2008/2008-sp-reportviolations.html.

enforcing the various statutes. In certain circumstances, some of the pollution control statutes make specific distinctions with regard to major and minor emitters/dischargers. A designation of "major" generally applies to those entities that, because of their size or operations, have the potential to have a significant impact on the environment. Most of the statutes and accompanying regulations include authorities for reducing the stringency, and in some cases providing exemptions from regulatory requirements to minimize their impacts on small businesses and operations.

There is no readily available, current, comprehensive list and description of the complete universe of those who are regulated under all of the major pollution control statutes. EPA has been criticized for not adequately defining the regulated universe, a step that GAO determined to be a critical component necessary to evaluate the effectiveness of enforcement.[55] EPA-OECA compiled data regarding the size of the regulated community in September 2001, and estimated a total universe of more than 41 million.[56] Although cited by EPA subsequently from time to time, most commonly in strategic planning documents, the agency has not updated the estimate.

There are, however, data and information that provide some indications of the size and diversity of this universe—for example, in EPA's primary enforcement and compliance databases (see additional discussion in **Appendix A**). EPA's publicly available Enforcement and Compliance History Online (ECHO) provides for integrated searches of data for more than 800,000 facilities for compliance with CWA, CAA, and RCRA.[57] The data are primarily based on permitted facilities. Another EPA centrally managed database is the Facility Registry System (FRS), which primarily identifies "facilities, sites or places" subject to federal pollution control requirements; it contains more than 2.5 million unique facility records.[58] The FRS database is primarily based on permit information for CWA, CAA, and RCRA, but includes information reported regarding CERCLA sites. It does not include information indicating the universe regulated under other statutes. In yet another source, the ECOS indicated that states reported that more than 3 million regulated facilities required state agency oversight for environmental compliance in 2003.[59] The differences in the various sources are an indication of the difficulty involved in accurately and consistently tracking the size of the regulated populations.

EPA's various program offices (e.g., air, water, and waste) maintain and publish information and profiles regarding characterizations of regulated entities and their operations. Generally included are estimates of the types and amounts of emissions and discharges, or wastes being handled. For example, EPA's Office of Air and Radiation (OAR) maintains a national database of air emissions estimates for individual point- or major-source categories.[60] The database contains information on

---

[55] EPA-OIG, Limited Knowledge of the Universe of Regulated Entities Impedes EPA's Ability to Demonstrate Changes in Regulatory Compliance, 2005-P-00024, September 19, 2005 (http://www.epa.gov/oig/); and GAO, Human Capital: Implementing an Effective Workforce Strategy Would Help EPA to Achieve Its Strategic Goals, GAO-01-812, pp. 24-25, July 2001, http://www.gao.gov/docsearch/repandtest.html.

[56] EPA-OECA, *OECA Regulatory Universe Identification Table.* Internal EPA memorandum November 15, 2001, EPA-OIG, *Limited Knowledge of the Universe of Regulated Entities Impedes EPA's Ability to Demonstrate Changes in Regulatory Compliance*, 2005-P-00024, September 19, 2005, http://www.epa.gov/oig/.

[57] Enforcement and Compliance History Online (ECHO), http://www.epa-echo.gov/echo/about_site.html

[58] EPA, Federal Registry System (FRS) Overview, http://www.epa.gov/enviro/html/fii/index.html.

[59] ECOS, *State Environmental Contributions to Enforcement and Compliance 2000-2003*, June 2006, http://ecos.org/section/publications.

[60] EPA, *National Emissions Inventories for the U.S.*, http://www.epa.gov/ttn/chief/index.html.

---

stationary and mobile sources that emit common ("criteria") air pollutants[61] and their precursors, as well as hazardous air pollutants (HAPs).[62] The categories presented in these sources do not reflect 100% of the total number of facilities being regulated.

Another source for characterizing the sectors of the regulated community is EPA's "Sector Notebooks."[63] EPA has defined sectors as distinct parts of the economy that share similar operations, processes or practices, environmental problems, and compliance issues. EPA recognizes that there are likely a number of circumstances where regulated entities within specific geographic regions may have unique characteristics that are not fully reflected in the profiles contained in the sector notebooks. In addition, some of the notebooks were completed several years ago. Nevertheless, notebook profiles provide fairly comprehensive characterizations of key sectors included within the regulated community.

Table 2 lists industry and government sectors for which the agency has completed sector notebooks and developed compliance assistance tools.

Table 2. EPA Industry and Government Sectors

Available Sector Notebooks

Aerospace	Health Care	Printing
Agriculture	Local Government Operations	Prisons and Correctional Institutions
Automotive	Marinas	Pulp/Paper/Lumber
Chemicals	Metals	Ready Mix/Crushed Stone/Sand and Gravel
Computers/Electronics	Minerals/Mining/Processing	Rubber/Plastics
Construction	Paints and Coatings	Shipbuilding and Repair
Dry Cleaning	Petroleum	Textiles
Federal Facilities	Pharmaceuticals	Transportation
Food Processing	Ports	Tribal
Furniture	Power Generators	

Source: Table generated by CRS with information from EPA's Sector Compliance Assistance and Sector Notebooks website, http://www.epa.gov/comp iance/assistance/sectors/index.html.

---

[61] Under §106 of the Clean Air Act, EPA has set National Ambient Air Quality Standards for six principal pollutants classified by the EPA as "criteria pollutants": sulfur dioxide (SO2), nitrogen dioxide (NO2), carbon monoxide (CO), ozone, lead, and particulate matter.

[62] Under §112 of the Clean Air Act, EPA is to establish technology-based emission standards, called "MACT" standards, for sources of 188 pollutants listed in the legislation, and to specify categories of sources subject to the emission standards.

[63] For more information regarding EPA's Sector Compliance Assistance and Sector Notebooks, see http://www.epa.gov/compliance/assistance/sectors/index.html.

Enforcement at Federal Facilities[64]

Unless a statutory exemption exists, federal facilities are subject to the federal pollution control statutes,[65] and generally also must adhere to the environmental laws and regulations of the states and municipalities in which they are located, to the same extent as others in the regulated community. EPA reported that it concluded 57 enforcement actions against federal agencies for alleged violations of federal pollution control laws during 2011, resulting in an estimated reduction of more than 713,000 pounds of pollutants.[66] This is compared to 52 enforcement actions, resulting in an estimated reduction of more than 311,000 pounds of pollutants during FY2010.[67] Federal agencies are also subject to relevant requirements of executive orders.[68]

In FY2011, approximately $9.0 million in penalties were assessed for federal facility violations and violators agreed to invest an estimated $5.0 billion in cleanup and improved operations to comply with environmental laws, compared to $749,000 assessed penalties and investment of an estimated $163 million in FY2010.[69]

Regulating federal facilities under pollution control laws presents certain unique challenges. Although all are potentially subject to pollution control laws and regulations, a majority of federal agencies and their facilities are not involved in activities that would generally warrant compliance requirements. According to EPA, facilities operated by DOD and DOE make up a significant portion of the universe of "major" federal facilities.[70] Major federal facilities generally refer to those facilities that, because of their size or operations, have the potential to have a significant impact on the environment. Compliance/enforcement information for DOD and DOE is reported individually, while other federal agencies are generally categorized together as Civilian Federal Agencies.[71]

---

[64] See EPA, "Compliance and Enforcement at Federal Facilities," http://www.epa.gov/compliance/federalfacilities/index.html.

[65] Most federal environmental laws contain provisions that subject federal facilities to federal, state, and local requirements, and allow such facilities to be sued just as a nongovernmental entity. In addition, such provisions generally grant the President authority to exempt federal facilities from such requirements when in the "paramount interest" or (less commonly) the "national security interest" of the United States. See Clean Air Act (42 U.S.C. §7418), Clean Water Act (33 U.S.C. §1323), Resource Conservation and Recovery Act (42 U.S.C. §6961), and Safe Drinking Water Act (42 U.S.C. §300j-6). A more limited federal facility provision and presidential exemption is found in the Comprehensive Environmental Response, Compensation and Liability Act (42 U.S.C. §9620). The Toxic Substances Control Act nowhere expressly states that federal facilities are subject to the statute, but nonetheless does authorize presidential exemptions (15 U.S.C. §2621). For discussion of exemptions, particularly as they pertain to DOD, see CRS Report RS22149, *Exemptions from Environmental Law for the Department of Defense (DOD)*, by David M. Bearden.

[66] EPA-OECA, *Compliance and Enforcement Annual Results 2011 Fiscal Year Federal Facilities*, http://www.epa.gov/compliance/resources/reports/endofyear/eoy2011/programs/federalfacilities.html.

[67] EPA-OECA, *Compliance and Enforcement Annual Results 2010 Fiscal Year Federal Government Compliance*, http://www.epa.gov/compliance/resources/reports/endofyear/eoy2010/fedfacilities.html.

[68] For examples of executive orders with directives addressing environmental management at federal facilities, see EPA's *Federal Facilities Sector Notebook A Profile of Federal Facilities*, EPA 300-B-96-03, January 1996, pp. 2-11 and 2-12, available at http://www.epa.gov/compliance/assistance/sectors/index.html.

[69] See footnote 66 and footnote 67.

[70] EPA Federal Facilities Enforcement Office, *The 2008 State of Federal Facilities An Overview of Environmental Compliance at Federal Facilities*, EPA 305-R-09-001, August 2009; and *The State of Federal Facilities An Overview of Environmental Compliance at Federal Facilities FY 2005-2007*, EPA 305R08002, September 2008, http://cfpub.epa.gov/compliance/resources/reports/accomplishment/federal.cfm?templatepage=4.

[71] See footnote 70.

The major federal pollution control laws provide EPA with authorities to enforce requirements and impose penalties at federal facilities that are not in compliance. The Federal Facility Compliance Act of 1992 specifically amended RCRA to clarify that DOD and all other federal facilities are subject to penalties, fines, permit fees, reviews of plans or studies, and inspection and monitoring of facilities in connection with federal, state, interstate, or local solid or hazardous waste regulatory programs.[72] The SDWA includes similar language regarding federal facilities, but most of the other federal environmental laws do not include such specific provisions. CERCLA (Superfund) Section 120 requires federal agencies with NPL sites to investigate and clean up the contamination, and significantly contaminated federal facility sites have been listed on EPA's National Priorities List (NPL).

Whether other pollution control laws should be amended to clarify their applicability to federal facilities has been an issue of debate in Congress.

Enforcement Response and Compliance Tools

EPA and states apply a set of environmental enforcement tools to identify and correct noncompliance, restore environmental damage, and impose penalties intended to deter future violations. Compliance with pollution control laws is addressed through a continuum of response mechanisms, ranging from compliance assistance to administrative and civil enforcement, to the stronger criminal enforcement. The spectra of tools, which escalate in terms of their level of severity and intensity, are authorized in each of the environmental statutes. The following sections of this report provide a brief overview of the various enforcement response mechanisms.

Over the years, EPA and states have sought to effectively balance the provision of guidance and assistance to prevent violations or achieve compliance by regulated entities with federal pollution control requirements, with the imposition of strong enforcement actions in response to violations. Some critics have depicted environmental enforcement as overly litigious, or requiring unwarranted remedies. Others counter that actions are not pursued with enough rigor and frequency, or that penalties are not severe enough to deter noncompliance. EPA officials have countered that, in some instances, the agency is relying more on settlements and focusing on requiring increased expenditures on pollution control technologies, and that it is focusing judicial actions on larger and more complex cases that are expected to result in larger environmental benefits.

EPA and states maintain a considerable degree of flexibility in determining how to respond to potential violations, to the extent authorized by individual statutes. Initially, a potential violation is identified through monitoring, inspecting, citizen reporting, or through self-reporting by the regulated entity. As a first step in the enforcement process, unless an imminent danger or hazard has been determined, EPA and states may attempt to obtain corrective actions by simply issuing a warning or notifying a facility that minor violations may exist, and granting reasonable time for compliance. EPA or a state may then (or sometimes as a first step) initiate a civil administrative action under its own authority without involving the judicial process, or file formal civil or criminal[73] judicial actions in court.

---

[72] 42 U.S.C. §6961.

[73] When persons willfully or knowingly disregard the law.

Sanctions imposed, whether through negotiated settlements or decisions by the court, generally include required actions to achieve compliance and to correct environmental damage (injunctive relief), and may include monetary penalties (and incarceration in the case of criminal violations). During the last 10 years, settlements increasingly have also included requirements that violators undertake mutually agreed-upon environmentally beneficial projects supplemental to other sanctions.[74]

As noted, EPA, states, and the courts have considerable discretion in determining sanctions and remedies on a case-by-case basis so that the individual circumstances of each case are appropriately addressed. A majority of environmental violations are addressed and resolved administratively by states and EPA, and many of these cases are settled through negotiations between the government and the alleged violator. For example, during FY2011, EPA issued 1,324 administrative compliance orders and filed 1,830 final administrative penalty order complaints. In comparison, during FY2011, 148 civil judicial cases were filed with the court, and 180 civil judicial enforcement cases were concluded.[75] Civil judicial cases constitute the second-largest category of environmental enforcement actions. Historically, judicial actions focused on violation of a single environmental statute. In recent years, EPA and states have increased the frequency of reliance on a multimedia (multi-statute) approach and multimedia investigations.

The number of administrative and judicial enforcement actions and penalties often fluctuate significantly from year to year. These fluctuations are generally a reflection of a combination of factors, including statutory deadlines; new or amended requirements in response to new scientific information or amended and new regulations; increased or decreased resources; environmental priority changes at the federal or state levels; and increased or improved monitoring/reporting. For example, EPA reported that the number of administrative penalty order complaints issued by the agency more than doubled, from 2,229 complaints in FY2005 to 4,647 in FY2006, then declined to 2,237 in FY2007, 2,056 in FY2008, 1,914 in FY2009, 1,901 in FY2010, and 1,735 in FY2011.[76] The combined $152.0 million in civil penalties (administrative and judicial) assessed in FY2011 were the highest in the last five fiscal years.[77] Additionally, the total dollar amount of penalties collected in a given year could reflect the completion of one or two large cases. For example, EPA reported that a single case accounted for 62% of the total civil penalties assessed for FY2004. Illustrations of the frequency of enforcement actions by type over time are presented in **Appendix B**; this appendix also includes illustrations of administrative and judicial penalties assessed over time by statute.

Monitoring, Inspections, and Evaluations

Critical steps in enforcing environmental laws include the compilation of monitoring data, and inspection and evaluation of the activities of the regulated community to determine who is complying with applicable regulatory requirements and permit conditions, and who is not. Compliance monitoring, evaluations, and investigations all serve to identify violations and

---

[74] See the discussion later in this report on Supplemental Environmental Projects (SEPs).

[75] See *Compliance and Enforcement Annual Results 2011 Fiscal Year, End of Year Data and Trends Accomplishments*, http://epa.gov/compliance/resources/reports/endofyear/eoy2011/eoy-data.html.

[76] EPA OECA, *Data Planning and Results Annual Results*, http://epa.gov/compliance/data/results/annual/index.html.

[77] See *Compliance and Enforcement Annual Results 2011 Fiscal Year, End of Year Data and Trends Analysis and Trends*, http://epa.gov/compliance/resources/reports/endofyear/eoy2011/eoy-trends.html.

provide insights into potential priority issue areas that may need to be addressed more broadly. Monitoring and reporting can be both media program-based (e.g., air, water, waste) and sector-based (e.g., industrial, mobile source, utilities), and are often included in permit requirements. Data reported and obtained, as well as observations and evidence collected by inspectors, enable EPA and states to identify specific environmental problems and determine whether a facility is in compliance. The information and evidence could eventually be used in an enforcement action. The mere collection of information or threat of inspection itself often creates an awareness of the regulators' interest, and can encourage compliance.

EPA identifies several forms of compliance monitoring that are used differently by the agency and states, depending upon the statute, the nature of the pollutants, and the types of facilities being regulated:

- **Self-Monitoring/Reporting:** Most environmental laws require (typically through permitting) regulated entities/facilities to monitor and record their own compliance status and report some or all of the tracking results to the responsible regulating authority. In addition to informing the regulators, self-monitoring also allows a company to measure its performance and evaluate its strategies for achieving or maintaining compliance.

- **Review of Records:** Regulatory agencies review data and information reported or otherwise compiled and collected.

- **Full and Partial Inspections/Evaluations:**[78] Individual facility environmental inspections, conducted by EPA regional staff and the states, are the primary tool used by regulators for initial assessment of compliance. Through sampling, emissions testing, and other measures, inspections examine environmental conditions at a facility to determine compliance (or noncompliance) with specific environmental requirements, and to determine whether conditions present imminent and substantial endangerment to human health and the environment. Inspections/evaluations can be conducted all at once or in a series of partial inspections.

- **Area Monitoring:** Area monitoring looks at environmental conditions in the vicinity of a facility, or across a certain geographic area. Examples of methods used for area monitoring include ambient monitoring and remote sensing.

According to EPA's most recent reported trends data, a total of 19,000 EPA enforcement inspections and evaluations were conducted under the various statutes during FY2011.[79] Although most inspections are carried out by the states, annual data for the total number of inspections conducted by states are not readily available due to data-reporting variability and other limitations. Based on a subset of states surveyed, ECOS reported that roughly 136,000 compliance inspections were conducted by states in 2003 for the major federal environmental programs—air, drinking water, surface and groundwater, hazardous waste, and solid waste.[80] The total number of inspections reported by ECOS does not account for all inspections conducted by

---

[78] The CWA requires evaluations instead of investigations, which include reviewing reports, records, and operating logs; assessing air pollution control devices and operations; and observing visible emissions or conducting stack tests.

[79] See footnote 77.

[80] The Environmental Council of the States (ECOS), "State Environmental Agency Contributions to Enforcement and Compliance: 2000-2003," June 13, 2006.

states under federal pollution control programs—for example, inspections under FIFRA are not included. In reports to EPA by states under the Pesticide Enforcement Grant program, states, tribes, and territories reported between 90,000 and 100,000 FIFRA inspections each fiscal year for FY2006 through FY2008. These FIFRA activities, typically administered by states' departments of agriculture, are not reflected in the EPA or the ECOS totals.

To put the ECOS number of inspections into perspective, in 2003, the ECOS survey identified 440,000 regulated facilities under these five major environmental programs. EPA's Facility Registry System (FRS), which identifies facilities and sites subject to federal environmental regulation, currently contains unique records for more than 2.5 million facilities (see the above discussion under the heading Regulated Community). **Appendix B** presents data on the number of inspections conducted annually by EPA over time.

Civil Administrative Actions

As noted earlier, a majority of environmental pollution control violations are addressed and resolved administratively by states and EPA without involving a judicial process. EPA or a state environmental regulatory agency may informally communicate to a regulated entity that there is an environmental problem, or it may initiate a formal administrative action in the form of a notice of violation or an Administrative Order to obtain compliance. An Administrative Order imposes legally enforceable requirements for achieving compliance, generally within a specified time frame, and may or may not include sanctions and penalties.

An initial step in the enforcement process is often a Notice of Violation, or in some instances, a warning letter. Warning letters are issued mostly for first-time violations that do not present an imminent hazard. These notifications are intended to encourage regulated entities to correct existing problems themselves and come into compliance as quickly as possible. According to EPA, in many cases, these notices are not escalated to further formal enforcement action because a facility corrects problems and returns to compliance in response to the notice.

Through administrative enforcement actions, EPA and states may (1) require that the violator take specific actions to comply with federal environmental standards, (2) revoke the violator's permit to discharge, and/or (3) assess a penalty for noncompliance. As indicated previously, administrative actions frequently end in negotiated settlements. These mutually agreed-upon resolutions are typically in the form of a Consent Agreement or Final Administrative Order/Penalty. According to EPA's FY2011 annual results, during FY2011, EPA initiated 1,324 administrative compliance orders and 1,760 administrative penalty order complaints. EPA imposed penalties in 1,735 final administrative penalty orders during FY2011, representing a total value of $47.9 million.[81]

Federal administrative orders are handled through an administrative adjudicatory process, filed before an administrative law judge (ALJ), or, in the regions, by EPA's regional judicial officers (RJOs). The EPA Office of Administrative Law Judges (OALJ) is an independent office within the agency.[82] ALJs, appointed by the EPA Administrator,[83] perform adjudicatory functions and

---

[81] See footnote 75.

[82] Administrative Procedure Act, 5 U.S.C. §557.

[83] 5 U.S.C. §3105.

render decisions in proceedings between EPA and individuals, entities, federal and state agencies, and others, with regard to administrative actions taken to enforce environmental laws and regulations. RJOs, designated by each of the EPA Regional Administrators,[84] perform similar adjudicatory functions in the EPA regions. Decisions issued by ALJs and RJOs are subject to review and appeal to the Environmental Appeals Board (EAB), which also functions independently of EPA.[85] Environmental Appeals Judges are appointed by the EPA Administrator.[86] Federal pollution control laws and regulations specify who may raise an issue before the EAB, and under what circumstances. EAB decisions often involve reviews of the terms of federal environmental permits and the amount of assessed financial administrative penalties.

Civil Judicial Enforcement

After civil administrative enforcement actions, civil judicial cases constitute the next-largest category of environmental enforcement. These are lawsuits filed in court against persons or entities who allegedly have not complied with statutory or regulatory requirements, or, in some cases, with an Administrative Order. Authorities for pursuing civil judicial actions and penalties are specified in each of the individual environmental statutes. Civil judicial cases are brought in federal district court by DOJ on behalf of EPA, and, for the states, by State Attorneys General. Not all of the cases referred to DOJ are filed with the court. The length of a civil case from its initiation to completion is highly variable, often extending across several years and sometimes across different presidential administrations. Like administrative enforcement actions, many civil judicial actions end as negotiated settlements, typically in the form of Consent Decrees. During FY2011, EPA-OECA referred 232 civil judicial cases to DOJ; 148 civil judicial complaints were filed with the court; and 182 cases were concluded (cases filed prior to and during FY2011).[87]

Criminal Judicial Enforcement

States and EPA may initiate criminal enforcement actions against individuals or entities for negligent or knowing violations of federal pollution control law. Criminal actions are especially pursued when a defendant knew, or should have known, that injury or harm would result. Knowing criminal violations of pollution control requirements are considered deliberate, and not the result of accident or error.

In addition to the imposition of monetary fines and requirements to correct a violation and restore damages, conviction of a criminal environmental violation can result in imprisonment. EPA reported that 371 new environmental crime cases were opened during FY2011,[88] 7.2% more than the 346 criminal cases opened in FY2010.[89] Authorities for pursuit of criminal actions vary under each of the statutes. For example, under the SDWA (42 U.S.C. §300h-2(b)), the criminal violations must be deemed willful—that is, they were committed with intent to do something

---

[84] Title 40 CFR Part 22 Subpart A §22.4(b).

[85] Title 40 C.F.R. Part 22 Subpart A §22.8.

[86] Title 40 C.F.R. §1.25(e). EAB judges are Senior Executive Service ("SES")-level career agency attorneys (U.S. EPA, *The Environmental Appeals Board Practice Manual*, June 2004, available at http://www.epa.gov/eab/pmanual.pdf).

[87] See footnote 75.

[88] See footnote 75.

[89] See footnote 76.

prohibited by that law; the CWA (33 U.S.C. §1319(c)) authorizes criminal sanctions against those who have knowingly or negligently violated that statute.

Recent examples of criminal actions include the illegal disposal of hazardous waste; importation of certain banned, restricted, or regulated chemicals; the export of hazardous waste without prior notification or permission of the receiving country; the removal and disposal of regulated asbestos-containing materials inconsistent with requirements of the law and regulations; tampering with a drinking water supply; and negligent maintenance resulting in discharge of hazardous materials.[90]

The EPA-OECA Office of Criminal Enforcement, Forensics, and Training (OCEFT), the office to which the agency's criminal investigators are primarily assigned, oversees implementation of the agency's federal environmental crimes investigation program. Within DOJ, the U.S. Attorneys Offices and ENRD's Environmental Crimes Section (ECS) prosecute criminal cases and work closely with EPA's OCEFT investigators.

State and local law enforcement agencies and their environmental protection-related agencies, and other federal agencies, are also often key participants in federal environmental criminal actions. To facilitate investigations and cases, environmental crime task forces have been established nationally.[91] These task forces are composed of representatives from federal (including representatives from DOJ-ECS and special agents from EPA), state, and local law enforcement, and environmental regulatory enforcement. The FBI, DOT, Coast Guard, Fish and Wildlife Service, Army Corps of Engineers, SEC, IRS, and other relevant federal agencies also may play significant roles.

An increased emphasis on criminal enforcement of the pollution control laws occurred in the mid-1970s with the issuance of extensive guidelines for proceeding in criminal cases, and in 1981 with the creation of an Office of Criminal Enforcement and the hiring of criminal investigators in EPA's regional offices. During the late 1980s, criminal environmental enforcement was further enhanced when Congress conferred full law enforcement powers upon EPA criminal investigators as part of the Medical Waste Tracking Act of 1988 (18 U.S.C. §3063). Further, under Title II of the Pollution Prosecution Act of 1990 (P.L. 101-593), Congress authorized the appointment of a director of a new Office of Criminal Investigations within EPA, and mandated the hiring of 200 criminal investigators by FY1996.[92]

Staffing levels of criminal investigators at EPA have been of interest to some Members, particularly during deliberations on appropriations. For example, the 1990 Pollution Prosecution Act (P.L. 101-593) required EPA to hire and maintain 200 criminal investigators. A provision in the House-passed FY2008 Interior and Environmental Agencies Appropriations bill (H.R. 2643) would have required EPA to bring the total number of investigators up to the level of 200 as

---

[90] For criminal case highlights for FY2010, see EPA's compliance and enforcement annual results website at http://epa.gov/compliance/resources/reports/endofyear/eoy2010/criminal/index.html. See also EPA's Criminal case Activities website at http://www.epa.gov/Compliance/resources/cases/criminal/major.html.

[91] For a listing of EPA's Criminal Investigation Division Offices and associated Environmental Crimes Task Force Teams nationwide, see http://www.epa.gov/Compliance/criminal/intergovernmental/environcrimes.html.

[92] For a historical perspective of EPA's criminal enforcement, see *EPA Review of the Office of Criminal Enforcement, Forensics, and Training*, November 2003, http://www.epa.gov/Compliance/resources/publications/criminal/oceft-review03.pdf.

statutorily required.[93] The provision was not included in the FY2008 appropriations (P.L. 110-161, Title II of Division F). Congressional concerns regarding staff and funding for EPA's criminal (and civil) enforcement were also expressed in conference report language accompanying EPA appropriations for FY2003 through FY2005,[94] and were the topic of a congressionally requested EPA-OIG investigation.[95]

EPA's criminal enforcement agents are authorized law enforcement officers who, in addition to investigating federal environmental statutes, investigate U.S. Criminal Code (Title 18) violations often associated with environmental crimes, such as conspiracy, false statements, and interfering with federal investigations. As noted, Congress has been concerned with the staffing of criminal investigators.

Table 3 below shows the number of EPA investigators assigned to the criminal enforcement program for FY1997 through FY2013 (projected), as reported by EPA.[96] The number of EPA special agents went from about 50 in 1990 to more than 200 by 1998.[97] As of September 2007, the number of EPA investigators had dropped to 168; this decline was an issue of concern in Congress and elsewhere. As a result of an EPA/OECA three-year hiring strategy to increase the number of criminal investigators, the number of investigators increased to 183 in FY2008, 186 in FY2009, and 206 in FY2010. The total number of criminal investigators declined to 202 in FY2011 and EPA expects the current 192 inspectors on board will be 191 by the end of FY2012, and anticipates this number will remain constant in FY2013.[98]

---

[93] Title VI—Additional General Provisions §605 of H.R. 2643 (June 28, 2007, placed on the Calendar of the Senate). See also H.Amdt. 441 to H.R. 2643, offered and agreed to, June 26, 2007, inserted under Title VI—Additional General Provisions §601 (CR H7221-H7222). The FY2008 omnibus appropriations (P.L. 110-161) did not include this general provision (Joint Explanatory Statement Accompanying Division F of the Consolidated Appropriations Act for FY2008 (P.L. 110-161, H.R. 2764), as presented in the *Congressional Record*, December 17, 2007, p. H16142).

[94] Conference Report (H.Rept. 108-792, p. 1563) accompanying the Consolidated Appropriations Act, 2005, P.L. 108-447; Conference Report (H.Rept. 108-401, p. 1126) accompanying the Consolidated Appropriations Act, 2004, P.L. 108-199; and Conference Report (H.Rept. 108-10 , p. 1445) accompanying Consolidated Appropriations Resolution, 2003, P.L. 108-7.

[95] See footnote 9.

[96] Based on information provided directly to CRS by EPA's Office of Congressional and Intergovernmental Relations, October 31, 2007, March 26, 2008, April 4, 2010, August 15, 2011, and June 20, 2012, and EPA's *Compliance and Enforcement Annual Results for 2010 Criminal Enforcement*, http://www.epa.gov/compliance/resources/reports/endofyear/eoy2010/criminal/index.html#agents.

[97] See footnote 92.

[98] See footnote 96.

Table 3. Number of EPA Criminal Investigators: FY1997-FY2013

Fiscal Year	Number of Investigators
1997	200
1998	200
1999	192
2000	179
2001	181
2002	217
2003	217
2004	202
2005	189
2006	183
2007	168
2008	183
2009	186
2010	206
2011	202
2012	191 est.
2013	191 est.

Source: Prepared by CRS with data provided by EPA's Office of Congressional and Intergovernmental Relations, October 31, 2007, March 26, 2008, April 4, 2010, August 15, 2011, and June 20, 2012, and EPA's *Compliance and Enforcement Annual Results for 2010: Criminal Enforcement*, http://www.epa.gov/compliance/resources/reports/endofyear/eoy2010/criminal/index.html#agents.

Note: The number of agents listed for 2002-2004 includes investigators who performed a mix of environmental crimes and homeland security work. The number of agents in FY2005 and FY2006 includes a cumulative total of 1.5 FTEs for specialized national security event response training of 25 agents so they can be deployed, if needed, to respond to a national security event.

In FY2009, EPA opened the "EPA Fugitives" website, which provides photographs and information about alleged violations of individuals who have avoided prosecution for allegedly committing environmental crimes.[99] The site solicits assistance from the public and from law enforcement agencies to help locate identified environmental "fugitives," and provides guidance on how to report information related to the fugitives' identity and/or current location. EPA reported that creditable reports received through the website assisted in the arrest or capture of three fugitives and the surrender of two others during FY2009; four were sentenced and one awaits trial.[100] Comparable information regarding "EPA Fugitives" was not reported by EPA in its FY2010 or FY2011 Annual Results;[101] however, the agency indicated that information obtained through the "Report a Violation" website[102] during FY2010 contributed to the opening of seven active criminal investigations, one of which resulted in an indictment.[103] EPA did not report any similar direct correlations with the "Report a Violation" website in its FY2011 annual results.

Sanctions[104] and Penalties

Sanctions and penalties imposed for violation of federal environmental pollution control laws have been of interest to some in Congress and the topic of a recent EPA-OIG report.[105] Settlements often require that violators achieve compliance and remedy environmental damages (injunctive relief). Monetary penalties may be included. Sanctions can also include permanent or temporary closure of facilities or specific operations, increased monitoring/reporting, revocation of existing permits or denial of future permits, and barring of receipt of federal contract funding or other federal assistance.[106] The settlement-required corrective and compliance actions, and the monetary penalties (and possibly incarceration for criminal violations), are intended to correspond directly with the specific violations (noncompliance) and the extent (or "gravity") of action committed.

Monetary penalties collected by the federal government as a result of an environmental enforcement agreement, order, or decision, are deposited with the U.S. Treasury.[107] However, under CERCLA (Superfund) and CWA, money recovered for the costs of replacing or restoring natural resources is used to restore the resources.[108] In the December 11, 2008, *Federal Register*,[109] EPA published its modifications to civil violation penalties in a final rule revising

---

[99] "EPA Fugitives," http://www.epa.gov/fugitives/.

[100] "EPA Fugitive Highlights," http://www.epa.gov/compliance/resources/reports/endofyear/eoy2009/2009criminalfugitives.html.

[101] See footnote 120.

[102] See discussion under the "Citizens" heading earlier in this report.

[103] EPA, *Compliance and Enforcement Annual Results for FY2010 Criminal Enforcement*, http://www.epa.gov/compliance/resources/reports/endofyear/eoy2010/criminal/index.html#engage.

[104] In the context of this report, "sanctions" refer to adverse consequences imposed in response to noncompliance.

[105] EPA-OIG, *EPA Needs to Improve Its Recording and Reporting of Fines and Penalties*, Report No. 10-P-0077, March 9, 2010, http://www.epa.gov/oig/reports/enforcement.htm.

[106] 2 CFR Part 180, 2 CFR Part 1532, and Executive Order 12549. Debarment is also authorized following criminal conviction under Clean Water Act (§508) and Clean Air Act (§306). See information regarding EPA's suspension and debarment program at http://www.epa.gov/ogd/sdd/debarment.htm.

[107] Under the Miscellaneous Receipts Act (31 U.S.C. §3302(b)), all court, or administratively imposed penalties must be paid by the government official receiving the monies to the U.S. Treasury.

[108] See, for example, 33 U.S.C. §1321(f)(5).

[109] U.S. EPA, "Civil Monetary Penalty Inflation Adjustment (Final) Rule," 73 *Federal Register* 75340-75346, (continued...)

---

statutory penalties at 40 C.F.R. Parts 19 and 27. The final rule increased most of the penalties by adjusting for inflation under the Debt Collection Improvement Act of 1996,[110] and also corrects previous calculation errors made during EPA's 2004 revisions to the penalties. The December 2008 rule adjusted the maximum penalty under section 203(a)(3)(B) of the Clean Air Act, and under the Toxic Substances Control Act and the Federal Insecticide, Fungicide, and Rodenticide Act.

States may have the explicit administrative authority to impose penalties under individual federal statutes. For example, the Safe Drinking Water Act requires (unless prohibited by a state's constitution) administrative penalty authority for states in certain dollar amounts as a condition of obtaining and/or retaining primacy for the Public Water System Supervision (PWSS) Program (§1413 (a)(6)).[111] As of June 2012, 55 of 57 states and territories had primacy authority for the PWSS program.[112] Although authorized under several of the other federal pollution control laws, EPA has not required—and not all states have obtained—administrative penalty authority. In some states, unlike the federal government, penalties obtained (or shared) as a result of an environmental enforcement action can be used to directly fund activities for environmental agencies and programs in the state, and not always to fund the state's general treasury.

In certain cases where the federal government has led the enforcement action, a state or states involved in the action may "share" resulting civil monetary penalties to the extent that the division is permitted by federal, state, and local law. A number of critical factors must be considered in accordance with EPA guidance[113] when determining division of penalties, including the state's active participation in prosecuting the case and its authority to collect civil penalties. EPA's guidance emphasizes that an agreement to include a division of civil penalties with states must be completed prior to issuance of a final settlement (order or consent decree).

The several statutes establish various factors to be considered in determining penalties: (1) the magnitude of environmental harm and the seriousness or gravity of a violation; (2) the economic benefit or gain to the violator as a result of illegal activity (noncompliance), including the gaining of a competitive advantage by the delaying or avoidance of pollution control expenditures that have been incurred by those in compliance; (3) violation history of the violator; and (4) in some circumstances, the ability of the violator to pay. Other factors, such as the degree of cooperation by the violator, whether the violation is self-reported, or the extent to which immediate action has been taken by the violator to mitigate potential harm, may also be considered. Precedents in previous cases involving similar violations are also a consideration when determining penalties.

The federal pollution control statutes include civil administrative and judicial penalty assessment authority and limits, which are to be considered by ALJs or the courts in determining the

---

(...continued)

December 11, 2008, http://www.epa.gov/compliance/resources/policies/civil/penalty/penaltyinflationrule-frnotice121108.pdf

[110] Section 4 of the Federal Civil Penalties Inflation Adjustment Act of 1990, 28 U.S.C. 2461 note, as amended by the Debt Collection Improvement Act of 1996 (DCIA), 31 U.S.C. 3701, requires each federal agency to adjust statutory civil monetary penalties for inflation every four years under the laws administered by that agency.

[111] SDWA, 42 U.S.C. §300g-2(a)(6), added by SDWA Amendments of 1996 (P.L. 104-182).

[112] See page 6 of CRS Report RL31243, *Safe Drinking Water Act (SDWA) A Summary of the Act and Its Major Requirements*, by Mary Tiemann.

[113] EPA guidance for the "Division of Penalties with State and Local Governments," memorandum from Courtney M. Price, Assistant Administrator for Enforcement and Compliance Monitoring, October 30, 1985.

appropriate penalty. **Figure B-3** in **Appendix B** presents examples of dollar amounts of civil administrative, civil judicial, and criminal penalties assessed by EPA for the 20-year period FY1991-FY2011. According to EPA, a significant portion of the total annual dollar amount of all penalties assessed often reflects penalties assessed in a few cases, and, in some years, a single case. For example, EPA reported that a major RCRA case accounted for 26% of the total value of civil penalties reported in FY2006, and that, in FY2005, penalties assessed in a single RCRA corrective action case accounted for 53% of the reported assessed civil penalties for the year.[114]

EPA and DOJ have established several policies and guidelines to be considered by counsel when negotiating agreements and setting penalties.[115] EPA-OECA has also developed five computer models for calculating economic advantage, costs of Supplemental Environmental Projects (SEPs; see discussion under "Supplemental Environmental Projects (SEPs)," below), and for measuring the ability to afford compliance requirements and penalties.[116] The latter models vary depending on whether a violator is an individual, municipality, individual facility, or business entity (small business, large corporation, or conglomerate partnership). Findings of limited ability or inability to pay are one factor under which an enforcement case may be settled for less than the economic benefit of noncompliance. The models are to be used in conjunction with the policies and guidelines for calculating civil penalties.[117] The available models are:

- BEN, for calculating economic advantage/savings from avoidance of compliance;

- ABEL, for measuring a noncompliant entity's (e.g., a corporation's) ability to afford compliance and cleanup, and civil penalties;

- INDIPAY, for measuring an individual violator's ability to afford compliance and cleanup, and civil penalties;

- MUNIPAY, for measuring a noncompliant municipality's ability to afford compliance and cleanup, and civil penalties; and

- PROJECT, for calculating cost to a violator of undertaking a SEP (see the discussion regarding SEPs later this report).

Penalties Assessed to Federal Facilities[118]

Most federal pollution control statutes contain a provision expressly subjecting federal facilities to federal (and state and local) environmental regulation, and waiving sovereign immunity (thereby allowing federal agencies to be sued by nonfederal entities). Further, many federal

---

[114] EPA, Office of Enforcement and Compliance Assurance, *FY2006 OECA Accomplishments Report*, Spring 2007, EPA-300-R-07-001, http://cfpub.epa.gov/compliance/resources/reports/accomplishment/details.cfm.

[115] For example, EPA's revised *Consolidated Rules of Practice* ("CROP") (64 FR 40138, July 23, 1999) contains procedural rules for the administrative assessment of civil penalties, issuance of compliance or corrective action orders, and the revocation, termination or suspension of permits, under most environmental statutes. See EPA's web page, *Civil Penalty Policies*, at http://cfpub.epa.gov/compliance/resources/policies/civil/penalty/.

[116] U.S. EPA, Enforcement Economic Models, http://www.epa.gov/compliance/civil/econmodels/.

[117] Additionally, see EPA, *Guidance on Calculating the Economic Benefit of Noncompliance by Federal Agencies*, issued on February 13, 2006, Memorandum from Granta Y. Nakayama, Assistant Administrator, Office of Enforcement Compliance and Assurance, http://www.epa.gov/Compliance/resources/policies/federalfacilities/enforcement/cleanup/guid-econ-ben-noncomp-2-13-06.pdf.

[118] Prepared by Robert Meltz, Legislative Attorney, American Law Division.

environmental statutes authorize (or arguably authorize) EPA, states, and local governments to assess civil monetary penalties against federal agencies. (The Supreme Court rejected state authority to do so under the CWA.)[119] DOJ has issued opinions concluding that the CAA and RCRA underground storage tank provisions give EPA authority to assess civil money penalties against federal facilities. However, DOJ limits these conclusions to *administrative* assessment of penalties. Citing its constitutional theory of the "unitary executive," DOJ has historically refused to allow EPA to enforce *judicially* against other federal agencies, though case law has consistently been to the contrary. In contrast with EPA enforcement, there is no longer serious doubt that the Constitution allows states and other nonfederal entities to use the citizen suit provisions in federal environmental statutes to judicially enforce those laws against federal facilities.

During FY2011, EPA concluded 57 enforcement actions against federal facilities, and assessed $9.0 million in penalties. Federal agencies committed to invest more than $5.0 billion in FY2011 to improve their facilities and operations to remedy (clean up) past violations, to comply with federal laws, and to prevent future violations/pollution.[120]

Supplemental Environmental Projects (SEPs)

In addition to requiring violators to achieve and maintain compliance, and imposing appropriate sanctions and penalties, enforcement settlements may also include Supplement Environmental Projects (SEPs).[121] SEPs are projects that provide environmental and human health benefits that a violator may voluntarily agree to undertake in exchange for mitigation of penalties. A project must be related to the violation, and cannot be an activity the violator is legally required to take to achieve compliance. Penalties are to be mitigated by a SEP only during settlement negotiation, prior to imposition of the final penalty.

EPA has established a SEPs policy and developed guidance for their legal requirements and applicability, and has specified eight categories of acceptable projects.[122] These include pollution prevention, public health, and emergency and preparedness planning. EPA reported that 103 civil settlement cases during FY2011 included SEPs at an estimated value of $25.0 million.[123]

The incorporation of SEPs into enforcement actions became more common during the last decade, particularly by federal regulators, because of the potential for direct environmental benefit from such projects, versus the use of a monetary fine or penalty alone. Some states with administrative penalty authority have also employed the use of SEPs in their settlements.[124] Although these projects are required to be supplemental to other requirements, some contend that, in practice, inclusion of SEPs may result in lower monetary fines. The extent to which specific SEPs may have resulted in reduced monetary fines and penalties is not easily calculable.

---

[119] *U.S. Dept. Of Energy v. Ohio*, 503 U.S. 607 (1992).

[120] EPA-OECA, *Compliance and Enforcement Annual Results 2011 Fiscal Year Program Highlights Federal Facilities*, http://www.epa.gov/compliance/resources/reports/endofyear/eoy2011/programs/federalfacilities.html.

[121] For more information regarding SEPs, see http://www.epa.gov/compliance/civil/seps/index.html.

[122] Policy and guidance documents related to EPA's Supplemental Environmental Projects Policy are available at http://cfpub.epa.gov/compliance/resources/policies/civil/seps/.

[123] EPA-OECA, *Compliance and Enforcement Annual Results 2011 Fiscal Year End of Year Data Trends 2011 Accomplishments*, http://www.epa.gov/compliance/resources/reports/endofyear/eoy2011/eoy-data.html.

[124] The Environmental Council of States (ECOS), *State Environmental Agency Contributions to Enforcement and Compliance 2000-2003*, June 2006.

Environmental Justice and Enforcement/Compliance

Environmental justice (EJ) has been an area of debate among industry and public interest groups, and ongoing concern highlighted in congressional hearings and legislation. For example, an administrative provision included in the Omnibus Appropriations Act, 2009 (P.L. 111-8, Title II), specified that none of the funds made available by this act may be used in contravention of, or to delay the implementation of, Executive Order No. 12898 relating to federal actions to address environmental justice in minority populations and low-income populations.[125] On August 4, 2011, the White House announced the signing of a Memorandum of Understanding (MOU) on Environmental Justice and E.O. 12898 by the heads of 17 federal agencies.[126] The MOU included a Charter to add more structure and efficiency to the Federal Interagency Working Group on Environmental Justice; processes and procedures to more efficiently assist communities, and guidance for agencies to better coordinate their EJ activities; and various commitments each agency will be responsible for meeting. Discussion of the full scope of issues and concerns regarding environmental justice is beyond the scope of this report. However, the following discussion briefly highlights environmental justice in the context of enforcement and compliance.

The terms "environmental justice (or injustice)" and "environmental equity (or inequity)" may be interpreted broadly to describe the perceived level of fairness in the distribution of environmental quality across groups of people with different characteristics. In this sense, the environmental impact of any human activity might be evaluated to determine the distribution of environmental amenities and risks among people categorized according to any population characteristic, including gender, age, race, place of residence, occupation, income class, or language. In the political context, however, emphasis generally is more on the distribution of health risks resulting from exposure to toxic substances in residential or occupational environments of different racial, ethnic, or socioeconomic groups.

The 1994 Executive Order 12898, Federal Actions to Address Environmental Justice in Minority Populations and Low-Income Populations, directs each federal agency to "make achieving environmental justice part of its mission."[127] EPA is the federal agency with lead responsibility for implementing the executive order. EPA's Office of Environmental Justice (OEJ), located in OECA, is responsible for coordinating efforts to include environmental justice into policies and programs across the agency's headquarters and regional offices.[128] EPA's OEJ provides information and technical assistance to other federal agencies for integrating environmental

---

[125] Executive Order 12898, 49 *Federal Register* 7629, February 16, 1994, http://www.archives.gov/federal-register/executive-orders/1994.html.

[126] Executive Office of the President, Council on Environmental Quality, August 4, 2011, Press Release, Memorandum of Understanding (MOU) on Environmental Justice and E.O. 12898, http://www.whitehouse.gov/administration/eop/ceq/Press_Releases/August_04_2011. A copy of the MOU is available at http://epa.gov/environmentaljustice/resources/publications/interagency/ej-mou-2011-08.pdf See also EPA's "Federal Interagency Working Group on Environmental Justice," http://www.epa.gov/compliance/ej/interagency/index.html.

[127] See footnote 125.

[128] EPA's Office of Civil Rights (OCR) is responsible for the agency's administration of Title VI of the Civil Rights Act of 1964, including processing and investigating administrative complaints under implementing regulations (40 C.F.R. Part 7) prohibiting EPA-funded permitting agencies from "... permitting actions that are intentionally discriminatory or have a discriminatory effect based on race, color, or national origin." See http://www.epa.gov/civilrights/t6home.htm.

---

justice into their missions, engages stakeholders to identify issues and opportunities, and administers EPA environmental justice grants.[129]

EPA incorporated Environmental Justice in its FY2011-FY2015 Strategic Plan as the Cross-Cutting Fundamental Strategy "Working for Environmental Justice and Children's Health."[130] EPA has initiated implementation of "Plan EJ 2014," a strategy for expanding its efforts to integrate environmental justice into its various programs and strengthen "the Agency's effort to improve the environmental conditions and public health in overburdened communities."[131] At the time this CRS report was updated, EPA was soliciting comment through July 6, 2012, on an "informational publication" entitled *Creating Equitable, Healthy, and Sustainable Communities: Strategies for Advancing Smart Growth, Environmental Justice, and Equitable Development.*[132]

EPA's OEJ developed the Environmental Justice Strategic Enforcement Assessment Tool (EJSEAT).[133] EJSEAT remains a draft tool in development for internal EPA use only. OECA expects to use EJSEAT to "consistently identify possible environmental justice areas of concern," where potentially disproportionately high and adverse environmental and public health burdens exist, and assist EPA in making "fair" enforcement and compliance resource deployment decisions.[134] OEJ published a "Toolkit for Assessing Potential Allegations of Environmental Injustice," primarily to assist agency staff in assessing allegations of environmental injustice.[135] Citizens can evaluate overlap between environmental conditions and demographic characteristics by using EPA's EJView (formerly Environmental Justice Geographic Assessment Tool).[136]

Compliance Assistance and Incentive Approaches

A frequent criticism regarding implementation and enforcement of federal environmental requirements has been an emphasis, historically, on a "command and control" approach. In response to these criticisms, since the 1990s EPA and states have relied increasingly on compliance assistance to help the regulated community understand its obligations to prevent violations and reduce the need for enforcement actions, as well as to assist violators in achieving

---

[129] EPA reports that, since 1994, more than $23.0 million has been awarded to nearly 1,300 community-based organizations, and local and tribal organizations in the form of Environmental Justice Small Grants. For more information regarding EPA's Environmental Justice Program activities, see http://www.epa.gov/compliance/environmentaljustice/index.html, for information on these grants and other environmental justice grants and cooperative agreements.

[130] EPA, FY2011-2015 Strategic Plan as submitted to Congress and OMB on September 30, 2010, http://www.epa.gov/ocfo/plan/plan.htm.

[131] EPA, DRAFT Plan EJ 2014 was released July 27, 2010. In March 2011, EPA published nine draft Implementation Plans for accomplishing the goals of Plan EJ2014, http://www.epa.gov/compliance/environmentaljustice/plan-ej/index.html.

[132] Available at http://www.epa.gov/smartgrowth/equitable_development_report.htm.

[133] EPA-OECA, "Environmental Justice Strategic Enforcement Assessment Tool (EJSEAT)," http://www.epa.gov/environmentaljustice/resources/policy/ej-seat.html.

[134] See footnote 133.

[135] EPA-OECA, Office of Environmental Justice, EPA 300-R-04-002, http://www.epa.gov/environmentaljustice/resources/policy/ej-toolkit.pdf.

[136] EPA-OECA, *EJView*, http://www.epa.gov/compliance/environmentaljustice/mapping.html.

compliance. Many states have advocated compliance assistance and developed assistance programs designed to address specific environmental issues at the local level.[137]

EPA's Office of Compliance (OC) within OECA has introduced a number of compliance assistance programs, many of them developed in conjunction with support from the regions, states, and tribes.[138] Each EPA region has a designated Compliance Assistance Coordinator who serves as an "expert" within the region on compliance assistance priorities, strategies, and performance measurement. The coordinators work with subject-matter experts in the regions and at headquarters in the development of compliance assistance guides and workshops, and contribute to other assistance activities such as conducting compliance assistance visits.[139]

In addition to providing compliance assistance across the individual pollution control statutes, sector-based assistance is also provided. Developed and introduced in partnership between EPA, states, academia, environmental groups, industry, and other agencies, the National Compliance Assistance Centers provide sector-specific assistance.[140] There are currently 16 sector-specific web-based compliance assistance centers. As shown in **Table 4** below, the sector-specific centers include agriculture, auto repair, chemical manufacturing, federal facilities, and local governments.

Table 4. Sector Web-Based Compliance Assistance Centers

Sectors	
Agriculture	Food Processing
Automotive Recycling	Healthcare
Automotive Repair	Local Government
Border Compliance	Metal Finishing
Chemical Manufacturing	Paints and Coatings
Colleges/Universities	Printed Wiring Board Manufacturers
Construction	Printing
Federal Facilities	Tribal Governments

Source: Table created by CRS with information from the National Compliance Center website, available at http://www.assistancecenters.net/.

The use of compliance incentive approaches has been evolving. Incentives generally are policies and programs that may reduce or waive penalties and sanctions under specific conditions for those who voluntarily take steps to evaluate, disclose, correct, and prevent noncompliance. Examples include self-disclosure programs and related tools such as environmental audit protocols, Environmental Management Systems, and other innovation projects and programs designed to achieve environmental benefits.

[137] ECOS, State Agency Contributions to Enforcement and Compliance, ECOS 01-004, April 2001.

[138] For more information regarding EPA's compliance assistance programs, see http://www.epa.gov/compliance/assistance/index.html.

[139] EPA-OECA, http://www.epa.gov/Compliance/assistance/planning/index.html.

[140] For more information regarding the National Compliance Assistance Centers, see http://www.epa.gov/compliance/assistance/centers/index.html or http://www.assistancecenters.net/.

One of the earliest formal EPA incentive approaches is the EPA Audit Policy—"Incentives for Self-Policing: Discovery, Disclosure, Correction and Prevention of Violations"—in effect since 1995.[141] Under the policy, certain violations are voluntarily reported after being discovered through self-audit. In many cases EPA eliminates civil penalties, and may offer not to refer certain violations for criminal prosecution. In early 2007, EPA solicited comments on the question of to what extent, if any, the agency should consider providing incentives to encourage new owners of recently acquired facilities to discover and disclose environmental violations, and to correct or prevent their reoccurrence.[142]

To further promote compliance through the use of various incentive approaches, EPA encouraged incentive approaches as part of its core program guidance included in the OECA FY2012[143] and FY2013[144] National Program Manager Guidance. The FY2013 guidance was distributed to Regional Administrators and State Environmental Commissioners in April 2012. However, EPA also continues to evaluate its various voluntary programs.

In March of 2009, for example, EPA notified participating stakeholders of its decision to discontinue the National Performance Track Program, which had been in place since July of 2000.[145] Designed as a private-public partnership to supplement EPA's existing regulatory activities, Performance Track encouraged facilities who met certain criteria[146] to voluntarily work toward environmental goals that were beyond the legal requirements. EPA reported that at the time of its termination on May 14, 2009,[147] the program had a total membership of nearly 547 facilities (including 82 new members in 2008) in 49 states and Puerto Rico. In her March 2009 memorandum to Performance Track stakeholders,[148] EPA Administrator Jackson announced her decision to halt the program "with the intent of refining those concepts that can lead us to a stronger system of environmental protection." EPA had conducted reviews of the Performance Track and the agency's environmental leadership programs in general.

---

[141] For more information regarding EPA's incentive programs and initiatives, see http://www.epa.gov/compliance/incentives/index.html.

[142] 72 *Federal Register* 27116, May 14, 2007.

[143] See footnote 23.

[144] See footnote 24.

[145] Memorandum from Lisa P. Jackson, EPA Administrator, to Performance Track Members, State Program Contacts, and Network Partners, March 16, 2009; and Memorandum from Charles W. Kent, Director of Cross-Media Programs, EPA's Office of Policy, Economics, and Innovation, to Performance Track Members, State Program Contacts, and Network Partners, March 25, 2009, http://www.epa.gov/performancetrack/index.htm. See also 74 *Federal Register* 22742 (May 14, 2009), http://www.epa.gov/performancetrack/downloads/PTtermination_notice5-14-09_74FR22741.pdf, and memorandum from Catherine R. McCabe, OECA Principal deputy Director, and Marcia E. Mulkey, Acting Associate Administrator, Office of Policy Planning and Compliance Assurance: Enforcement and Compliance Guidance on the termination of the National Environmental Performance Track Program, June 25, 2009, http://www.epa.gov/performancetrack/downloads/OECA-09-000-9690memo.pdf.

[146] According to EPA's Performance Track website, to be eligible for membership in the program, applicants must have "... implemented an independently assessed environmental management system, have a record of sustained compliance with environmental laws and regulations, commit to achieving measurable environmental results that go beyond compliance, and provide information to the local community on their environmental activities." Detailed criteria can be found at http://www.epa.gov/performancetrack/ (Note: As of October 2009, EPA no longer updates this information, but the link is still available as a reference or resource).

[147] See also *Performance Track Final Progress Report*, May 2009 on EPA's National Performance Track website, http://www.epa.gov/performancetrack/index.htm. (Note: as of October 20, 2009, the website is no longer being updated.)

[148] See footnote 145.

EPA's reliance on incentive approaches has been met with some skepticism by those who favor more traditional enforcement. Critics are concerned that incentive and voluntary approaches subtract resources from an already limited pool of enforcement resources. EPA and other supporters of these approaches contend that they result in cost savings by reducing burdens on investigators, achieve desired environmental improvements, and allow for the leveraging of additional resources through partnerships. Aspects of EPA's incentive approaches have been the subject of reviews by EPA-OIG and GAO.[149]

Funding for Enforcement/Compliance Activities

The adequacy of resources needed by EPA, DOJ, and the states to effectively enforce the major federal environmental pollution control laws is often highlighted during congressional debate of fiscal year appropriations. Historically, Congress has specified funding levels for certain aspects of EPA enforcement activities, or required the agency to undertake certain actions under annual appropriations; an example is the previously mentioned provision included in the House-passed FY2008 Interior and Environmental Agencies Appropriations bill (H.R. 2643) that would have required EPA to hire criminal investigators to bring the total number of investigators up to the statutory requirement of 200, pursuant to the Pollution Prosecution Act of 1990.[150] (The provision was not included in the FY2008 consolidated appropriations.)[151]

The President's FY2013 request include $615.9 million for EPA's enforcement activities, compared to $583.4 million enacted for FY2012, $593.5 million for FY2011, and $596.9 million for FY2010.[152] To date, Congress and the President have not completed action on any of the 12 regular appropriations acts for FY2012, which begins on October 1, 2011. **Table 5** illustrates the distribution of funding and full-time equivalents (FTEs) among various enforcement activities across the agency's appropriations accounts for the FY2013 President's request and the three prior fiscal years enacted. Because of differences from fiscal year to fiscal year in the scope of the activities included within each of the accounts, apt direct comparisons below the appropriations account level are often difficult. These differences include the addition and discontinuation of program activities, as well as the reorganization and consolidation certain activities.

---

[149] EPA-OIG: *Performance Track Could Improve Program Design and Management to Ensure Value*, Report No. 2007-P-00013, March 29, 2007. GAO: *Environmental Protection Challenges Facing EPA's Efforts to Reinvent Environmental Regulation*, RCED-97-155, July 2, 1997.

[150] Title VI—Additional General Provisions, §605 of H.R. 2643 as placed on the Calendar of the Senate (June 28, 2007).

[151] Joint Explanatory Statement Accompanying Division F of the Consolidated Appropriations Act for FY2008 (P.L. 110-161, H.R. 2764), as presented in the *Congressional Record*, December 17, 2007 (p. H16142).

[152] EPA's appropriations are within the jurisdiction of the Interior, Environment, and Related Agencies appropriations subcommittees.

Table 5. EPA-OECA's FY2010-FY2012 Enacted and FY2013 Requested Appropriation and FTEs by EPA Appropriations Account and Program Activity

(dollars in thousands)

EPA Appropriation Account / Program Activity	FY2010 Enacted		FY2011 Enacted		FY2012 Enacted		FY2013 Requested	
	Dollars	FTEs	Dollars	FTEs	Dollars	FTEs	Dollars	FTEs
Total	**$596,692.0**	**3,387.3**	**$593,488.0**	**3,370.6**	**$583,358.0**	**3,294.1**	**$615,884.0**	**3,273.6**
Environmental Programs Management (EPM)	**$365,748.0**	**2,256.1**	**$368,051.0**	**2,252.8**	**$361,997.0**	**2,220.1**	**$396,198.0**	**2,240.8**
Brownfields	$501.0	2.6	$479.0	$479.0	$478.0	2.6	$371.0	1.6
Civil Enforcement	$146,636.0	973.0	$180,668.0	$180,668.0	$177,465.0	1,184.0	$188,582.0	1,183.7
Comp iance Assistance and Centers	$25,622.0	167.1	—	—	—	—	—	—
Comp iance Incentives	$9,560.0	62.5	—	—	—	—	—	—
Comp iance Monitoring	$99,400.0	610.4	$106,874.0	629.7	$107,151.0	613.9	$125,209.0	631.7
Criminal Enforcement	$49,637.0	253.8	$50,236.0	253.8	$48,006.0	257.7	$51,775.0	264.2
Enforcement Training	$3,278.0	15.6	—	—	—	—	—	—
Environmental Justice	$7,090.0	28.9	$6,856.0	28.9	$6,841.0	28.8	$7,161.0	28.9
Geographic Program: Chesapeake Bay	$700.0	3.7	$3,126.0	3.2	$2,583.0	8.1	$3,437.0	8.2
Homeland Security (critical infrastructure protection)	$2,616.0	11.8	—	—	—	—	—	—
NEPA Implementation	$18,258.0	117.7	$17,592.0	117.5	$17,298.0	116.1	$17,424.0	113.5
Faci ities Infrastructure and Operations	$2,450.0	9.0	$2,220.0	9.0	$2,175.0	8.9	$2,239.0	9.0
Science and Technology (S&T)	**$15,351.0**	**90.5**	**$15,293.0**	**90.5**	**$15,265.0**	**89.6**	**$15,593.0**	**90.5**
Forensics Support	$15,351.0	90.5	$15,351.0	90.5	$15,265.0	89.6	$15,593.0	90.5
State and Tribal Assistance Grants (STAG)	**$23,810.0**	**—**	**$23,763.0**	**—**	**$23,725.0**	**—**	**$24,286.0**	**—**
Categorical Grant: Pesticides Enforcement	$18,711.0	—	$18,674.0	—	$18,644.0	—	$19,085.0	—
Categorical Grant: Toxics Substances	$5,099.0	—	$5,089.0	—	$5,081.0	—	$5,201.0	—
Categorical Grant: Sector Program	$0.0	—	$0.0	—	$0.0	—	$0.0	—

EPA Appropriation Account / Program Activity	FY2010 Enacted		FY2011 Enacted		FY2012 Enacted		FY2013 Requested	
	Dollars	FTEs	Dollars	FTEs	Dollars	FTEs	Dollars	FTEs
Leaking Underground Storage Tanks (LUST)	**$797.0**	**4.8**	**$789.0**	**4.8**	**$789.0**	**4.7**	**$792.0**	**4.8**
Comp iance Assistance and Centers	$797.0	4.8	—	—	—	—	—	—
Civil Enforcement			$789.0	4.8	$789.0	4.7	$792.0	4.8
Oil Spills Response	**$2,267.0**	**17.3**	**$2,423.0**	**17.3**	**$2,424.0**	**17.3**	**$3,110.0**	**18.1**
Civil Enforcement	$1,998.0	15.5	$2,288.0	16.4	$2,286.0	16.4	$2,968.0	17.2
Comp iance Assistance and Centers	$269.0	1.8	—	—	—	—	—	—
Comp iance Monitoring	—	—	$135.0	0.9	$138.0	0.9	$142.0	0.9
Hazardous Substances Superfund	**$188,719.0**	**1,018.6**	**$183,169.0**	**1,005.2**	**$179,158.0**	**962.4**	**$175,905.0**	**919.4**
Comp iance Assistance and Centers	—	—	—	—	—	—	—	—
Comp iance Incentives	—	—	—	—	—	—	—	—
Compliance Monitoring	$1,216.0	1.9	$1,234.0	1.9	$1,221.0	1.9	$1,223.0	1.9
Criminal Enforcement	$8,066.0	38.0	$8,090.0	38.0	$7,895.0	37.2	$7,680.0	34.0
Enforcement Training	$899.0	5.2	—	—	—	—	—	—
Environmental Justice	$795.0	4.0	$799.0	4.0	$583.0	3.9	$613.0	4.0
Forensics Support	$2,450.0	14.7	$2,396.0	14.7	$2,419.0	14.3	$1,214.0	5.7
Homeland Security (critical infrastructure protection)	$1,760.0	8.2	—	—	—	—	—	—
Superfund: Enforcement	$162,963.0	879.1	$160,888.0	879.1	$156,744.0	839.2	$156,583.0	819.6
Superfund: Federal Facilities Enforcement	$10,570.0	67.5	$9,762.0	67.5	$9,762.0	67.5	$10,530.0	59.3

Source: Compiled by CRS with data received from the Environmental Protection Agency's Office of Congressional and Intergovernmental Relations (OCIR) in written communications: August 15, 2011, and June 20, 2012. Differences from fiscal year to fiscal year in the scope of the activities included within each of the accounts make apt direct comparisons difficult below the appropriations account level. This includes adding or discontinuing program activities, as well as reorganizing and conso idating certair activities.

DOJ's resource (funding/staff) requirements and outlays associated with its litigation activities under the major federal pollution control statutes are, in the main, a subset of the funding (proposed and previously appropriated) for the Environment and Natural Resources Division (ENRD) in its annual budget justifications. As discussed previously, ENRD is responsible for the majority of DOJ's support of the federal pollution control laws, as well as many other responsibilities, including representing the United States in matters regarding natural resources and public lands, acquisition of real property by eminent domain for the federal government, and cases under wildlife protection laws.

The President's FY2013 budget request for DOJ included $110.4 million and 582 FTEs for ENRD. An additional $23.7 million for up to 115 FTEs included in the President's request for EPA was to be transferred to DOJ/ENRD through a reimbursable agreement for Superfund work. FY2012 enacted levels for ENRD were $108.0 million and 582 FTEs, plus $24.6 million for up to 115 FTEs transferred from EPA. Of the FY2012 enacted amount, including the transfers from EPA, roughly $69.6 million and 367 FTEs were for environmental litigation activities; $10.8 million and 57 FTEs were for criminal litigation conducted by DOJ's Environmental Crimes Section; and $58.8 million and 310 FTEs were for civil environmental enforcement and defensive litigation conducted by the Environmental Enforcement and the Environmental Defense Sections.[153]

Detailed reporting of federal funding to states and states' funding contributions for pollution control enforcement/compliance activities is not readily available. ECOS has tracked a broader category of state funding and expenditures that it defines as annual "environmental and natural resource spending," which, in more recent years, has been primarily based on survey data reported by states.[154] The data, which include state and federal funding, are limited for purposes of enforcement of federal pollution control laws in that they combine environmental and natural resource spending. Also, states vary in how they track and report this type of spending. The data do provide a source of state funding from a national perspective. In its March 2008 state expenditures report, ECOS only analyzed regulatory environmental agency work, which includes work pursuant to the primary federal pollution control laws addressed in this report and related activities. For FY2008 ECOS projected a total expenditure for all states combined of $12.65 billion for these regulatory environmental protection activities. ECOS reported that $3.06 billion, or less than 25% of the projected amount, was from federal funding to states for these purposes.[155] Based on a February 2010 survey of 36 states and Puerto Rico, ECOS reported that of the agencies represented by the survey respondents, 2,112 positions were eliminated or were being held vacant due to budget limitations in FY2010.[156]

---

[153] DOJ, Justice Management Division, Budget and Performance, *Department of Justice FY2013 Congressional Budget Submission* http://www.justice.gov/jmd/2013justification/, and information provided by DOJ ENRD staff in written communication to CRS, June 19, 2012. See also, *Budget Trend Data 1975 Through the President's 2003 Request to the Congress*, pp. 55-61, Spring 2002, http://www.usdoj.gov/archive/jmd/1975_2002/btd02tocpg.htm.

[154] ECOS, *ECOS Budget Survey Budgets are bruised, but Still Strong*, R. Steven Brown and Michael J. Kiefer, Summer 2003 *ECOStates*, http://www.ecos.org/section/states/spending.

[155] ECOS, *March 2008 Green Report State Environmental Expenditures, 2005-2008*, by R. Steven Brown, Executive Director, Environmental Council of the States, March 2008, http://www.ecos.org/files/ 3057_file_March_2008_Green_Report.pdf; see also ECOS' Publications on State Spending website at http://www.ecos.org/section/states/spending.

[156] ECOS, *March 2010 Green Report Impacts of Reductions in FY 2010 on State Environmental Agency Budgets*, March 2010 http://www.ecos.org/files/4011_file_March_2010_ECOS_Green_Report.pdf by Victoria Phillips, ARRA Reporting Manager, Massachusetts Department of Environmental Protection; see also ECOS' Publications on State (continued...)

In an August 2010 report,[157] ECOS found that

> "Overall, state environmental agencies' budgets have decreased from FY2009 to FY2011. That said, there is a budget increase from FY2009 to FY2010 among states that included SRF/ARRA [State Revolving Loan Funds/American Recovery and Reinvestment Act of 2009] administrative funds. There has been a slight overall drop in money coming from state general funds, while funds from the federal government have increased marginally, and funds from "other" sources, such as those raised through permitting fees, have remained relatively constant."

Federal appropriations, in particular allocations to states, for adequate staffing and effective enforcement of federal environmental statutes to protect human health and the environment, will likely continue to be an issue of concern.

Conclusion

Fully evaluating and measuring the overall effectiveness of current (and past) pollution control enforcement and compliance activities can be quite complicated. Discussion throughout this report highlights the difficulties inherent in characterizing the many facets of environmental enforcement at a macro level, and identifies many of the factors that may contribute to its perceived successes and shortcomings. However, several indicators do provide insight into a better understanding of the complexities associated with elements of enforcement, such as the vastness and diversity of the regulated community, the multiplicity of the activities and priorities across many regulating entities, and variability across statutes.

Since the establishment of EPA in 1970, Congress has been interested in a number of crosscutting issues associated with the enforcement of pollution control statutes and regulations, as reflected in provisions of enacted and amended environmental legislation over time. Congressional interest remains heightened, particularly with regard to the substance of intergovernmental relations, EPA-state relations, and fiscal requirements. Congress's involvement with these issues could take several directions. One likely result could be oversight hearings. Alternatively, relevant appropriations legislation may contain provisions or language regarding funding for specific enforcement activities.

Congressional interest might focus on statutory approaches to establish changes in the EPA-states' partnership, such as legislation similar to past proposals concerning refinement of the National Environmental Performance Partnership System (performance partnerships, or NEPPS) and the associated grants award process. Congress may also consider other statute-specific legislation to address other long-standing concerns that affect enforcement/compliance activities.

(...continued)

Spending website at http://www.ecos.org/section/states/spending. David Emme, Chief, Bureau of Administrative Services, Nevada Division of Environmental Protection; and Beth Graves, Senior Project Manager, Environmental Council of the States.

[157] ECOS, *August 2010 Green Report Status of State Environmental Agency Budgets, 2009-2011*, by R. Steven Brown, Executive Director, and Adam Fishman, Intern, Environmental Council of the States, August 2010, http://www.ecos.org/files/4157_file_August_2010_Green_Report.pdf; see also ECOS' Publications on State Spending website at http://www.ecos.org/section/states/spending

The regulated community, public interest groups, federal and state officials, and Congress are often divided on whether to pursue legislation that would further expand or constrain enforcement/compliance. They are similarly divided with respect to proposals that would expand states' authority for implementing and enforcing certain aspects of the major federal pollution control laws.

Views and congressional involvement with respect to these issues are likely to continue to evolve in the years ahead.

Appendix A. Enforcement/Compliance Databases and Examples of Reported Results

Enforcement/Compliance Databases and Reporting

Compliance monitoring data are used to manage the compliance and enforcement program, and to inform the public of enforcement actions taken and penalties imposed. EPA and the states collect and maintain compliance/enforcement data in many forms. According to EPA's OECA FY2006 Accomplishments Report, ECOS reported that states collect about 94% of environmental quality data contained in EPA's databases, primarily from state-issued permits and monitoring programs.[158] Information is often entered into multiple databases or transferred from state databases. Historically, the databases were often incompatible, making cross media/statute queries difficult. In recent years, EPA has been working to integrate several of the individual databases to allow more cross referencing of compliance data by regulators and to provide querying capabilities to the public.[159]

EPA developed a new web-based tool and interactive map that allows the public to obtain detailed information by location about the environmental pollution control enforcement actions taken at approximately 4,600 facilities.[160] Released in December 2009, the interactive maps show facilities in the United States where EPA concluded an enforcement action between October 1, 2008, and September 30, 2011 (FY2011). The maps are provided on EPA's Annual Results website.[161] The maps do not include environmental pollution control enforcement actions taken by state or local governments.

EPA compiles data from the various databases and provides various statistics in the form of annual accomplishment and multi-year trends reports.[162] Reporting has traditionally focused on statute-by-statute results, including actions initiated and concluded, and penalties and other sanctions assessed. The reliability and consistency of EPA and state databases, and how effectively the reported information can be used as an indicator of environmental progress and the impacts of environmental enforcement has been an issue of some debate, and questioned in reviews conducted by EPA-OIG[163] and GAO.[164] Critics contend, and EPA has long recognized,

---

[158] EPA, *FY2006 OECA Accomplishment Report*, EPA-300-R-07-001, Spring 2007, http://cfpub.epa.gov/compliance/resources/reports/accomplishment/details.cfm.

[159] For a more complete list and descriptions of EPA's enforcement/compliance databases, see http://www.epa.gov/compliance/data/systems/index.html.

[160] For more information see EPA's website "Questions About the Annual Results Maps," http://www.epa.gov/compliance/resources/reports/endofyear/eoy2010/2010-map-questionsabout html

[161] See EPA "Concluded Enforcement Cases Map for 2011 Fiscal Year http://www.epa.gov/compliance/resources/reports/endofyear/eoy2011/nationalmap.html

[162] See "EPA Results and Reports" at http://www.epa.gov/compliance/data/results/index.html.

[163] EPA-OIG *ECHO Data Quality Audit—Phase 2 results EPA Could Achieve Data Quality Rate with Additional Improvements*, Report No. 10-P-0230, September 22, 2010; *EPA Needs to Improve Its Recording and Reporting of Fines and Penalties*, Report No. 10-P-0077, March 9, 2010; *Overcoming Obstacles to Measuring Compliance Practices in Selected Federal Agencies*, Report No. 2007-P-00027, June 20, 2007; *EPA Performance Measures Do Not Effectively Track Compliance Outcomes*, Report No. 2006-P-00006; *Congressional Request on Updating Fiscal 2003 EPA Enforcement Resources and Accomplishments*, Report 2004-S-00002, all available at http://www.epa.gov/oig/.

[164] GAO report: *Drinking Water Unreliable State Data Limit EPA's Ability to Target Enforcement Priorities and* (continued...)

---

that while somewhat indicative of the failure to comply with environmental requirements, counting enforcement actions alone ("bean counting") does not provide a complete measure of the effectiveness of the national environmental enforcement/compliance program.

EPA has expanded its reporting by including estimates of environmental benefits (pollution reduction and impacts avoided) in its "Annual Results" for the most recent fiscal years.

Overview of Enforcement/Compliance Databases

A number of EPA's single- and multi-media national databases include enforcement and compliance data elements. While these databases are generally available to EPA staff, and in some cases state and local governments, most are not readily available to the public. The Enforcement and Compliance History Online, or ECHO, developed and maintained by OECA is the most prominent publicly accessible database. Introduced in 2003, ECHO queries provide a snapshot of the most recent three years of a facility's environmental compliance record, but are limited primarily to certain requirements under the CAA, CWA, and RCRA. EPA continues to expand the integration and capabilities of this and other databases. Finally, several state environmental agencies maintain additional information about compliance and enforcement (beyond what is reported to EPA systems).[165]

The following brief summaries of several of EPA's integrated national databases are a consolidation of descriptions provided on the agency's website:

Enforcement and Compliance History Online (ECHO)

ECHO is an interactive website that allows users to query permit, inspection, violation, enforcement action, informal enforcement action, and penalty information for individual or multiple facilities. Initial queries return a list of relevant facilities, each linked to a "Detailed Facility Report," indicating:

- whether a facility has been inspected/evaluated,

- occurrence and nature of violations (noncompliance),

- nature of enforcement actions (including penalties) that have been taken,

- contextual information about the demographics surrounding the facility.

- In FY2011 EPA added interactive maps tracking federal enforcement activities (http://www.epa-echo.gov/echo/maps/enfactions/state_map.html).

See http://www.epa-echo.gov/echo/index.html.

(...continued)

Communicate Water Systems' Performance, Report No. GAO-11-381 June 17, 2011, http://www.gao.gov/products/ GAO-11-381; GAO *Environmental Enforcement EPA Needs to Improve the Accuracy and Transparency of Measures Used to Report on Program Effectiveness*, GAO-08-1111R, September 18, 2008, http://gao.gov.

[165] Several states have provided direct links to related websites, which EPA posts on the ECHO website at http://www.epa-echo.gov/echo/more_state_data.html.

Envirofacts

Envirofacts provides public access to information about environmental activities, such as releases, permit compliance, hazardous waste handling processes, and the status of Superfund sites, which may affect air, water, and land anywhere in the United States. Data are retrieved from various EPA source databases. Users can develop online queries, create reports, and map results. See http://www.epa.gov/enviro/.

Facility Registry System (FRS)

FRS (a companion to the integrated facility searches in Envirofacts) can be used to create facility identification records, including geographical location, and to locate sites or places subject to environmental regulations or oversight (e.g., monitoring sites). Records are based on information from EPA program national systems, state master facility records, and data collected from EPA's Central Data Exchange. See http://www.epa.gov/frs/.

Integrated Compliance Information System (ICIS)

ICIS integrates data that are currently located in several separate data systems. ICIS contains information on federal administrative and federal judicial cases under the following environmental statutes: the CAA, CWA, RCRA, EPCRA, TSCA, FIFRA, CERCLA (Superfund), SDWA, and MPRSA. ICIS also contains information on compliance assistance activities conducted in EPA regions and headquarters. The web-based system enables states and EPA to access integrated enforcement and compliance data. The public can only access some of the federal enforcement and compliance information in ICIS by using the EPA Enforcement Cases Search and EPA Enforcement SEP Search through ECHO. See http://www.epa.gov/compliance/data/systems/icis/index html.

Integrated Data for Enforcement Analysis (IDEA)

IDEA maintains copies of EPA's air, water, hazardous waste, and enforcement source data systems that are updated monthly. An internal EPA database, IDEA uses "logical" data integration to provide a historical profile of inspections, enforcement actions, penalties assessed and toxic chemicals released, for EPA-regulated facilities. See http://www.epa.gov/compliance/data/systems/multimedia/idea/index.html.

Online Tracking Information System (OTIS)

OTIS is a collection of search engines which enables EPA, state/local/tribal governments and certain other federal agencies to access a broad range of data relating to enforcement and compliance. No public access is available. This web interface application sends queries and draws data from the IDEA (discussed above) system, which integrates facility data from different EPA databases. IDEA copies many EPA and non-EPA databases, and organizes the information to facilitate cross-database analysis. See http://www.epa.gov/compliance/data/systems/multimedia/aboutotis html.

A number of other databases, mostly for single media, also include compliance/enforcement data. Many of these databases are the basis for certain data elements in the various IDEA and OTIS integrated databases, and typically are not directly available to the public. Other databases include the Air Facility System (AFS); Permit Compliance System (PCS); Resource Conservation and Recovery Act Information System (RCRAInfo); National Compliance Data Base System and Federal Insecticide, Fungicide, and Rodenticide Act/Toxic Substances Control Act Tracking System (NCDB/FTTS); and Safe Drinking Water Information System/Federal (SDWIS/FED).

Although the information on the integrated systems does not represent "real time" data, it is updated once a month when OECA refreshes the source data systems. Additionally, EPA routinely makes improvements to existing aspects of OTIS and IDEA and often enhances the system by adding new search capabilities and tools. For example, during FY2011, EPA made improvements to search result displays for Drinking Water Enforcement Targeting Tool (ETT), updated the Data Verification Tool used by states, added drinking water enforcement information to OTIS. EPA is also currently beta-testing a new Toxic Release Inventory (TRI) Comparative Analysis Tool. Updates and improvements can be tracked on the OTIS website under the "What's New" link at http://www.epa-otis.gov/otis/whats_new.html.

For a more complete list and descriptions of EPA's enforcement/compliance databases, see EPA's "Compliance and Enforcement Data Systems" web page at http://www.epa.gov/compliance/data/systems/index.html.

Appendix B. Examples of Reported Enforcement Actions and Penalties Over Time

The following figures and tables provide examples of the type of enforcement data collected, compiled and reported over time. They are intended to show proportional relationships of the various types of enforcement actions (e.g., administrative vs. judicial) in a given year and by statute, not annual or long-term enforcement trends. To compare the reported activities from year to year requires more detailed information regarding the specific circumstances in those years. There can be significant variability from year to year in how data were reported and which entities reported. EPA has refined terms and definitions in the data elements from year to year. Other factors that result in variability include the introduction of new regulatory requirements in a given year, and fruition of statutory deadlines.

The figures presented below reflect longer-term data (15 to 20 years) through FY2011, whereas the tables generally provide data for the most recent five or six years, depending on the availability of data for the most recent fiscal year. Results are presented by action (e.g., administrative, civil judicial, criminal judicial), and where readily reported, for actions by statute (e.g., Clean Water Act, Clean Air Act).

Figure B-1. EPA Civil Judicial Referrals, Administrative Order Complaints, and Criminal Referrals, FY1992-FY2011

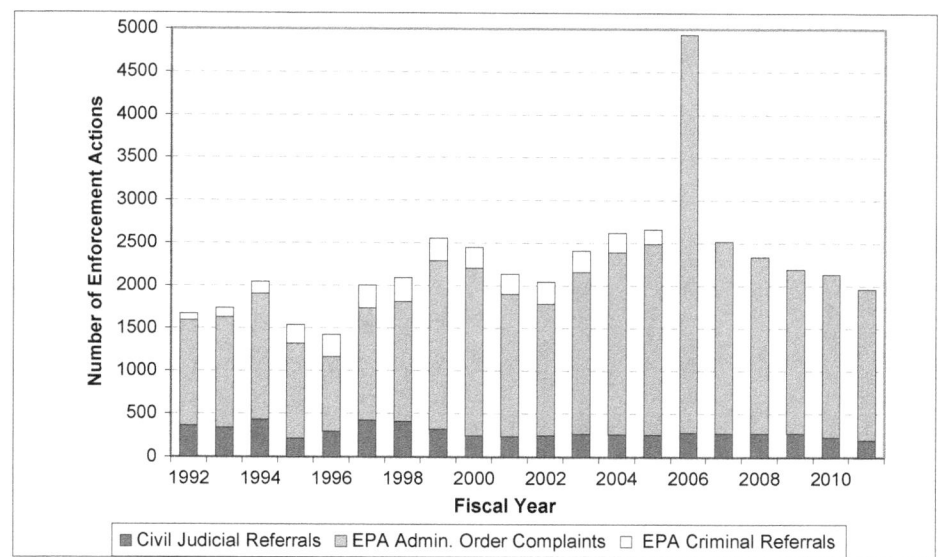

Source: Compiled by CRS using data from EPA's *National Enforcement Trends: EPA Long Term Trends*, as of October 2011, http://www.epa.gov/compliance/data/results/nets.html; *National Enforcement Trends (FY2004)—EPA Long Term Trends: Criminal Referrals and Penalties*, http://cfpub.epa.gov/compliance/resources/reports/nets/index.cfm; and EPA-OECA, *EPA Compliance and Enforcement Annual Results: 2011 Fiscal Year*, http://epa.gov/comp iance/data/results/annual/index.html. EPA terminated the count of criminal referrals as an internal Criminal Enforcement program measure in FY2005 and discontinued reporting these data in its trends reports.

Table B-1. EPA Civil Administrative, Civil Judicial, and Criminal Enforcement Actions, FY2006-FY2011

Enforcement Action	FY2006	FY2007	FY2008	FY2009	FY2010	FY2011
Administrative Comp iance Orders	1,438	1,247	1,390	1,588	1,302	1,324
Administrative Penalty Order Complaints	4,647	2,237	2,056	1,914	1,901	1,760
Final Administrative Penalty Orders	4,624	2,256	2,084	1,916	1,830	1,735
Civil Judicial Referral	286	278	280	277	233	199
Civil Judicial Cases Concluded	173	180	192	201	200	182
Criminal Judicial Referral	NR	NR	NR	NR	NR	NR
Criminal Judicial Cases Initiated (Opened)	305	340	319	387	346	371

Source: Compiled by CRS using data from EPA's *Compliance and Enforcement Annual Results FY2011, National Enforcement Long Term Trends: Enforcement Actions*, as of October 2011; also http://www.epa.gov/compliance/data/results/nets.html; and *National Enforcement Trends (FY2004)—Enforcement Actions: Criminal Enforcement Program Activities*, http://epa.gov/comp iance/data/results/nets.html.

Notes: NR = not reported. EPA terminated the count of criminal referrals as an internal Criminal Enforcement program measure in FY2005 and discontinued reporting these data in its trends reports.

Figure B-2. Number of EPA Federal Inspections and Evaluations by Statute, FY1995-FY2011

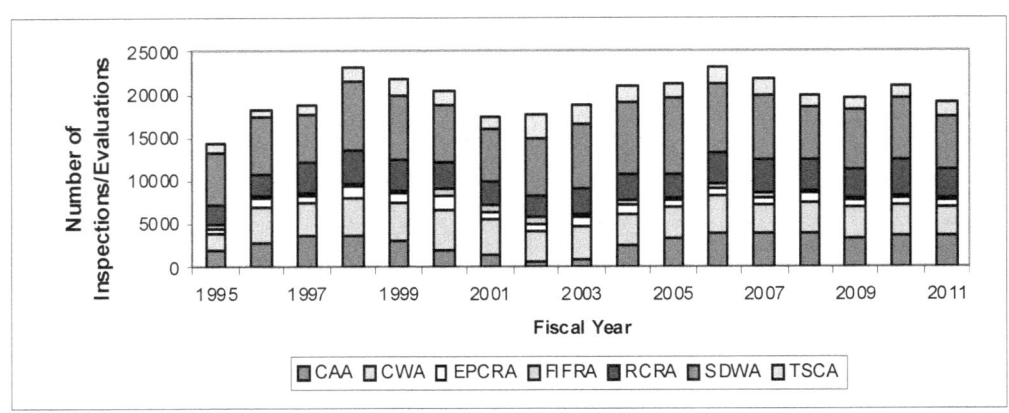

Source: Compiled by CRS using data from EPA's *National Enforcement Trends: EPA Long Term Trends: FY1994-FY2011 Federal Inspections and Evaluations,* as of October 2011, http://www.epa.gov/compliance/data/results/nets.html.

Table B-2. Number of EPA Enforcement Inspections and Evaluations by Statute, FY2006-FY2011

Statute	FY2006	FY2007	FY2008	FY2009	FY2010	FY2011
CAA	3,918	3,843	3,953	3,384	3,690	3,558
CWA	4,453	3,480	3,691	3,488	3,446	3,364
EPCRA	928	884	1,008	969	871	901
FIFRA	344	360	366	346	372	364
MPRSA	0	0	0	0	0	0
RCRA	3,812	3,874	3,477	3,171	4,231	3,181
SDWA	7,768	7,618	5,946	6,927	7,034	5,955
TSCA	2,008	1,662	1,441	1,439	1,368	1,640
Total	23,231	21,721	19,882	19,724	21,012	18,963

Source: Compiled by CRS using data from *EPA's National Enforcement Long Term Trends: EPA Inspections and Investigations,* as of October 2011, http://cfpub.epa.gov/compliance/resources/reports/nets/index.cfm, http://www.epa.gov/compliance/resources/reports/nets/nets-g2-inpectionslongterm.pdf. Totals may not add due to rounding.

CAA: Clean Air Act

CWA: Clean Water Act

EPCRA: Emergency Planning and Community Right-to-Know Act

FIFRA: Federal Insecticide, Fungicide and Rodenticide Act

MPRSA: Marine Protection, Research, and Sanctuaries Act

RCRA: Resource Conservation and Recovery Act

SDWA: Safe Drinking Water Act

TSCA: Toxic Substances Control Act

Figure B-3. Environmental Enforcement Penalties Assessed by EPA: Administrative, Civil Judicial, and Criminal, FY1990-FY2011

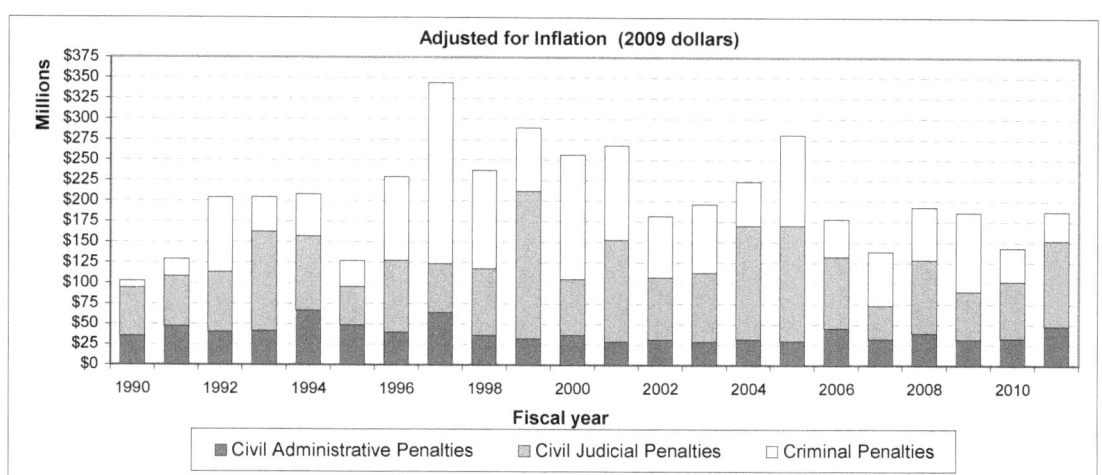

Source: Compiled by CRS using data from EPA's *Compliance and Enforcement Annual Results: 2011 Fiscal Year*, http://epa.gov/compliance/data/results/annual/index.html, *National Enforcement Trends—EPA Long Term Trends: FY1974-FY2011 Enforcement Penalties*, as of October 2010, http://www.epa.gov/comp iance/data/results/nets.html. Amounts converted to 2011 dollars using the GDP Chained Price Index from the Office of Management and Budget, *Budget of the U.S. Government for FY2011*, Historical Tables, http://www.gpo.gov/fdsys/browse/collectionGPO.action?collectionCode=BUDGET.

Table B-3. Environmental Enforcement Penalties Assessed by EPA: Administrative, Civil Judicial, and Criminal, FY2006-FY2011

(nominal dollars in thousands—not adjusted for inflation)

Fiscal Year	Administrative	Civil Judicial	Criminal[a]	Total
FY2006	$42,007	$81,808	$43,000	$166,815
FY2007	$30,696	$39,771	$63,000	$133,467
FY2008	$38,197	$88,356	$63,454	$190,108
FY2009	$31,609	$58,497	$96,000	$186,105
FY2010	$33,359	$70,249	$41,000	$144,600
FY2011	$44,881	$104,391	$35,000	$184,272

Source: Compiled by CRS using data from EPA's *Compliance and Enforcement Annual Results: 2011 Fiscal Year*, http://epa.gov/compliance/data/results/annual/index.html, and *National Enforcement Long Term Trends—Activities*, as of October 2011, http://www.epa.gov/comp iance/data/results/nets.html#longresults.

a. Criminal penalties represent fines and restitution.

Figure B-4. EPA Supplemental Environmental Projects: Number of Projects and Dollar Value, FY2000-FY2011

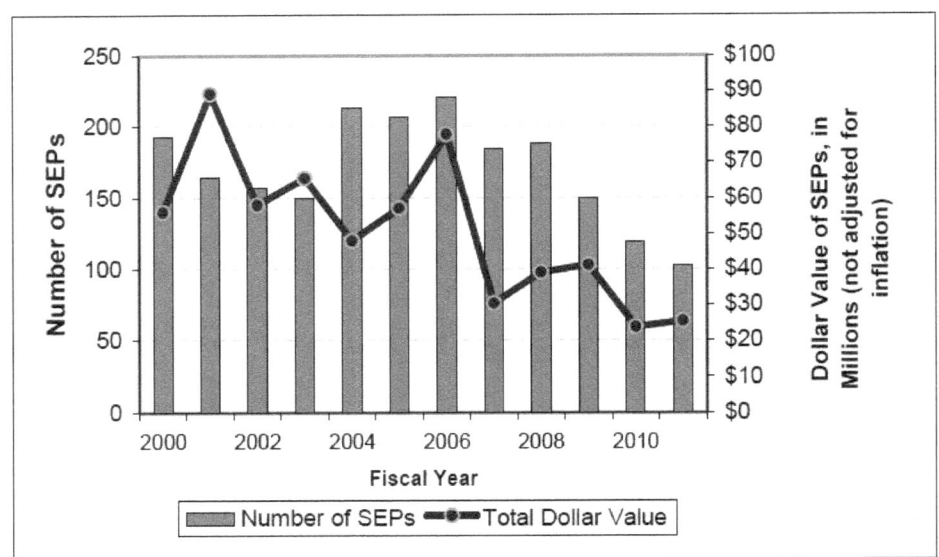

Source: Compiled by CRS using data from EPA's *Compliance and Enforcement Annual Results: 2011 Fiscal Year*, http://epa.gov/compliance/data/results/annual/index.html, and *National Enforcement Long Term Trends: FY1999-FY2011 Supplemental Environmental Projects*, as of October 2011, http://www.epa.gov/compliance/data/results/nets.html. http://www.epa.gov/comp iance/resources/reports/nets/nets-f4-seps.pdf.

Table B-4. Supplemental Environmental Projects (SEPs) Dollar Values as Reported by EPA: FY2006-FY2011

(dollars in thousands—not adjusted for inflation)

Statute	FY2006	FY2007	FY2008	FY2009	FY2010	FY2011
CAA	$41,712.9	$16,458.4	$15,679.8	$12,509.7	$8,160.0	$6,665.7
CERCLA	$2,732.8	$367.0	$1,306.6	$449.7	$174.8	$352.1
CWA	$21,712.8	$8,431.4	$13,904.6	$5,264.9	$12,419.0	$10,488.0
EPCRA	$1,208.2	$1,387.4	$1,066.1	$2,338.9	$736.7	$914.9
FIFRA	$31.1	$369.0	$637.4	$158.6	$46.0	$6.9
MPRSA	$0.0	$146.5	$0.0	$0.0	$37.5	$0.0
RCRA	$2,923.3	$1,720.8	$3,671.4	$7,123.7	$1,111.9	$4,946.3
SDWA	$133.1	$59.2	$1,428.0	$3.8	$325.0	$1,212.8
TSCA	$7,313.1	$1,405.0	$1,352.4	$13,281.8	$763.4	$800.1
Total	$77,767.3	$30,344.8	$39,046.1	$41,121.1	$23,774.3	$25,386.8

Source: Compiled by CRS using data from EPA's *National Enforcement Long Term Trends: FY1999-FY2011 Supplemental Environmental Projects*, as of October 2011, http://www.epa.gov/compliance/data/results/nets.html. Totals may not add due to rounding.

CAA: Clean Air Act

CERCLA: Comprehensive Environmental Response, Compensation, and Liability Act (Superfund)

CWA: Clean Water Act

EPCRA: Emergency Planning and Community Right-to-Know Act

FIFRA: Federal Insecticide, Fungicide and Rodenticide Act

MPRSA: Marine Protection, Research, and Sanctuaries Act

RCRA: Resource Conservation and Recovery Act

SDWA: Safe Drinking Water Act

TSCA: Toxic Substances Control Act

Author Contact Information

Robert Esworthy
Specialist in Environmental Policy
resworthy@crs.loc.gov, 7-7236